A. J Starkweather, S. Robert Wilson

Socialism

Being a Brief Statement of the Doctrines and Philosophy of the Social

Labor Movement

A. J Starkweather, S. Robert Wilson

Socialism
Being a Brief Statement of the Doctrines and Philosophy of the Social Labor Movement

ISBN/EAN: 9783337077990

Printed in Europe, USA, Canada, Australia, Japan

Cover: Foto ©Suzi / pixelio.de

More available books at **www.hansebooks.com**

No. 461. 2 10 Cents.

LOVELL'S LIBRARY

Vol. 9. No. 461. Nov. 29, 1884. Annual Subscription, $9.00.

SOCIALISM

BY

A. J. STARKWEATHER

AND

S. ROBERT WILSON

JOHN W. LOVELL COMPANY

BEING

*A BRIEF STATEMENT OF THE DOCTRINES AND
PHILOSOPHY OF THE SOCIAL
LABOR MOVEMENT*

BY

A. J. STARKWEATHER
AND
S. ROBERT WILSON

WITH AN INTRODUCTION BY
BURNETTE G. HASKELL

NEW YORK
JOHN W. LOVELL COMPANY
14 AND 16 VESEY STREET
1884

"Ye tell me that this struggle is hopeless. That answer proves YOUR cowardice and unfaith! Let the NEW ORDER come! For if it comprises but ten men of exalted character, fully conscious of all that their destiny has of the happy and the sublime in it, and firmly resolved to save Liberty or perish with it—Liberty WILL BE SAVED!"

MAXIMILIEN ROBESPIERRE.

———

"The great appear great to us, only because we are on our knees—let us rise!"

THÉROIGNE DE MÉRICOURT.

———

"And I, too, love Peace, but not the peace of Slavery."—DANTON.

———

PREFACE.

THE issuance of this work needs no statement of the reason for its publication. The demand for a popular hand-book, briefly and forcibly presenting the doctrines which, in the opinion of many of the best thinkers of the world to-day, are necessary of adoption to preserve our modern civilization, is self-evident. It is in response to this demand that the book is before you.

Every important phase of the great labor movement which now shakes the foundations of the world is here for the first time in one brief essay presented to the public. So immense a theme so briefly elucidated must necessarily be but suggestive. It is provocative of inquiry rather than an absolute answer to all criticism that it may challenge. It is rather the gage of war, the iron gauntlet thrown into the lists, than the full armored knight, prepared for battle, and serenely confident of victory.

It seems to us that it is the duty of all reformers to know the fundamental principles of justice, and that those principles forever remain the same. No matter whether the reform sought at the time be but a step, yet it ought to be a step toward the loftiest mountain tops of liberty, and not a mere movement, blind, though well meant, amid the brakes and brambles of the gulch and valley.

The thoughtful men of earth, the Children of Light, foresee that these questions can be decided finally and forever by no other means than by the sword of war. That the day of conflict draws ever nearer and nearer, and that conditions themselves will force the fight long before the peoples of the world see and know the truths upon which the advent of the newer and grander life must be founded, is no longer a contested, but an admitted fact.

It behooves us, then, to waste no precious moments in useless labor.   Let us bend every energy to the education of the people, that they may, when clangs the fateful hour, know how and where to strike for liberty or death.

SAN FRANCISCO, CALIFORNIA, September 1, 1884.

LEXICON.

The Socialistic propaganda having introduced several new words to the public, and having as well attached definite meanings to several others, it will not be out of place, and will certainly conduce to clearness, to define them here :

Society.

Modern "civilized" Society is divided into three classes, as follows :

The Aristocracy, consisting of those people in Europe who come of "gentle blood" and those in America who live upon inherited wealth—the *Drones*.

The Bourgeoisie, consisting of all of those who derive their living from rent, profit, or interest ; those in short who are not wage-workers, together with their hangers-on and allies—the *Robbers*.

The Proletariat, the working people of the world, those who really do the *work* and who receive in return for their labor a part of its worth called "wages"—the *Plundered Slaves*.

[The adjectives formed from these words are bourgeois, proletarian ; the singular nouns defining an individual of these classes are a bourgeois, a proletarian, a proletaire. Bourgeois is pronounced, boor-zhwau. Bourgeoisie is pronounced, boor-zhwau-zie.—The word "proletariat" meant originally, and still means, "the disinherited."]

The two former classes sustain the present method which governs the obtaining of a livelihood in this world, which is denominated the "Competitive System of Industry." By the aid of pulpit, press, and politician, owned by them, and because of the ignorance of the working people, this system is maintained.

SOCIALISM.

Socialism is defined by Webster as follows : " A better and more just system of government." A better definition is this : Socialism is the science of Justice applied to social conditions of mankind, its fundamental principle being that the right to labor and to receive the *full* value of that labor must be secured to every individual. [Note : It is to be regretted that the words Communism and Socialism by general custom have become almost synonymous. In point of fact, though generally so used, they are not synonyms.]

COMMUNISM.

Communism is that scheme of social regeneration which urges the establishment of a system which, based upon the family, will require from its members only what they are able to produce and will return to them whatever they wish to consume.

INDIVIDUALISM.

Individualism (that commonly known as the " Manchester " school) is that peculiar and anarchical, or want of, method of social association which now prevails. Its only rule is to let he who has the power, take, and he retain who can. [☞ *Individual Sovereignty* based upon Socialism is an entirely different affair and must *not* be confused with it.]

POLICY OF THE SOCIALISTS.

The Social, the Sexual, and the Religious questions are entirely different ones and should not be confused with each other. Socialists are interested in the first, and only deal with the second and especially the third when they place themselves in antagonism to our course upon the first. We maintain that social reform once accomplished, all others will easily and naturally follow.

Economic Terms.

Capital is the surplus remaining of the earnings of labor after all its needs have been supplied—*it is stored up labor*, or honestly earned property.

Capitalized Profits (familiarly and wrongfully known in the commercial world as "capital") is either the *unpaid wages of the producer*, or a forced tax upon the necessities of the consumer.   [In this book the ordinary word "capital" is used, the authors not desiring at this stage of the movement to confuse the mind of the reader ; by "capital" both here and in general literature "capitalized profits" is really meant.]

Property (honestly acquired ; stored-up labor) is sacred.

Profit (capitalized profits ; miscalled "property" and "capital") is the solidified fruits of a wholesale brigandage ; in brief, theft.

Rent is robbery.

Interest is an immoral and unjust tax extorted by a master from the necessities of the slave.

THE DEVELOPMENT OF AMERICAN SOCIALISM.

In Mr. H. M. Hyndman's scientific text-book on Socialism ("The Historical Basis of Socialism in England") he shows that the Golden Age of the English people (from A.D. 1350 to 1500) was chiefly marked by the fact that the producing classes were *really* free to contract for their labor and its reward; that they held the land, the implements, and the produce alike at their own disposal, subject only to certain well-defined payments to the master class; that, producing for their own use and not for profit, they had at hand the necessities of food, clothing, and shelter as a result of their own labor; and that no man could call upon them for labor or for battle save of their own free will.

After showing how fine, sturdy, honest, and independent the English of these days were, how well they were fed, housed, and clothed, and how superior in every sense they were to their miserable descendants of to-day, Mr. Hyndman sketches with a master hand the course of their decadence.

How the land and raw materials were torn from their grasp by the aggressions of the larger capitalists, how the workers were divorced from their tools and flung into large factories, and how, by division of labor and outside production for profit under the wage system, the producers were finally converted into the proletariat of the present time, could not have been better stated nor more clearly proven.

That this same course of events has been followed in every civilized land is undoubtedly a fact, although the superficial thought of the present day fails to grasp the

historical points which mark its progress to the real
student. That it is especially the case in America not
even so superficial a thinker as Professor Sumner will, I
think, deny after he shall have noted the facts which I
propose briefly to touch upon.

Socialism, which in brief is that science that insists
upon the worker having, first, free access to the materials
of production ; second, free use of the tools of production, and third, free use of the medium of exchange—this
Science of Justice can with right claim that in America,
the social conditions which ultimately in every land will
compel its adoption, have swept from point to point,
from phase to phase with a rapidity and force seen in no
other clime.

Never before in so short a period have the people of
any nation progressed through the barbaric, the tribal,
the feudal, and the commercial ages. And if the law of
analogous sequences holds good, never will be witnessed
so rapid a shaking off of the chains of Capitalism and
so glorious a birth into the realms of Social Freedom
as will be seen here, in these United States, within the
next decade.

The people of this land were once free, prosperous,
and happy. They are now miserable, poor, and enslaved. That the first was and why, that the second is
and the reason therefor, I hope to show.

It was not the *sangre azul* of the Visigothic race, nor
the daring of the Paladins, nor the courage of a daunt-
less chivalry that drove the frail fleets of the first settlers
of America from the olden home. No—it was the development at home of the modern competitive system.
The seizure of the land and tools had begun, men were
driven from their homes, shut out of an opportunity to
labor, and naturally and inevitably they sought a place
abroad where the means of subsistence could be obtained.

Had no hospitable America been open to them they
would have remained at home and—fought. But the
path was open, and instead of fighting they fled. That
some of the poorer, the more desperate, perhaps as well

the braver, *did* fight, will be remembered when we recall the English insurrections of the working people
between 1536 and 1568, especially that of Robert Kett
in 1549.*

The original colonists of America consisted mainly of
English, though Holland, Sweden, France, Scotland,
Ireland, and Germany were represented by men driven
over by the same economic causes as those developed in
England.

Placed on the shores of an unknown country, unpro-
vided with either food or shelter, the exiles found, however, an abundance of the first requisite of economic
freedom—raw material free to all. Land, wood, coal,
iron, stone, wild animals, fowl, and fish abounded for all
who wished to use them. To these they applied their
labor. The result was a state of society approximating
that of the English people of the "Golden Age"—dif-
fering from it only in that a greater amount of toil was a
necessity, owing to the undeveloped state of the country.

Had the colonies been left to themselves they would
soon have made themselves independent of the mother
land, by manufacturing their own tools of production
and actively engaging in the making of the articles
found necessary for their welfare. But the capitalist
classes of England had scented the game. In 1660 they
passed the "Navigation Acts." By these the colonists
were forbidden to send their products to any market
but England, they were not allowed to buy goods save
in England, and to crown all everything had to be carried in English vessels.

These restrictive laws throttled local manufacture and
compelled the settlers not only to pay an unjust tax on
the tools of production but prohibited them as well
from even using certain tools at all.

In 1674 the capitalist class of England, through their
Parliament, took another step. They laid heavy duties
on certain imported articles and passed severe statutes
to enforce the Navigation Acts.

Meanwhile in the Colonies a capitalist class had also
been developed from three causes. First, the seizure

* En passant, note : that *now*, there being at hand no new Americas
the grand revolution is imminent in every land.

of large tracts of land under grants from the crown, these tracts lying around the points of commercial vantage ; second, the working of large estates by slave labor, which was introduced by English capitalist speculators as early as 1620 ; and third, the use of the English medium of exchange, money, early substituted for rolls of tobacco employed by the first settlers to gauge the relative value of different productions. The seized lands, the slaves, and the money were absorbed by this newly formed capitalist class. The first furnished them with the raw material, the second (slaves) with the instruments of production, and the third with a medium of exchange. This last, following the example of their class at all times, they supplemented by a creation of their own, a system of notes, drafts, checks, bills, etc., thus providing themselves with a practically free medium of exchange, using which they could in a great measure do without the authorized governmental medium, money.

Thus occupying this position they were free, though their freedom meant the slavery of the mere producers, who thenceforth were used simply as "tools."

Unlike the producers, this commercial class was quick to see any invasion of its rights, and when their fellows in England laid a tax upon all deeds, notes, bills, checks, under the name of the "Stamp Act," they saw at once that it meant a limit to their right of a free medium of exchange ; and ultimate slavery of their fraction to the larger thieves at home.

They protested ; but finding protests of no avail, they fought. And into the battle with them they dragged the already growing proletariat and the large and comparatively independent agricultural classes.

The revolution of 1776 was clearly and absolutely a bourgeois affair. Not only its causes but its results evidence that it was so.

Its parallel in England was the conquest by William of Orange ; in France the revolution of 1789.

The actual physical conflict once begun let us do the American capitalists the credit to declare that they did not shirk their share of the burden.

It is no more than fair to admit that the overtures which were made at midnight in an open boat on the James River by a certain faction to the Pretender, looking to his assuming the American crown, were made without the knowledge of the main body of the class. Yet it is said that the proposition of crowning Washington was received secretly with great favor and only abandoned on Hamilton's representations that the people would never submit to the name of "King," and his subtile suggestion as to the change of nomenclature.

The revolution once accomplished, independence of the capitalist classes attained, the sole study of the rising bourgeoisie was to prevent the proletariat from asserting *their* rights to material, tools, and money, and to hold these factors of happiness in their own hands alone.

This task was easy for three reasons :

1. Millions of acres of unclaimed, unused land stretched to the westward, seemingly to be so, to the eyes of the poor, forever.

2. War had tired the workers out. They had no heart for further controversy, and were anxious to again devote their energies to labor on their own land.

3. The few real patriots who saw the trend of events and who alone had sufficient leisure, ability, and wealth to successfully contest their advancement were bribed, cajoled, hoodwinked, threatened, or removed from the scene of action. Among these were Thomas Paine, against whom were brought the batteries of religious intolerance, and Thomas Jefferson, who was sent out of the way in honorable exile as Minister to the Court of France.

The bourgeoisie were thus masters of the field. Under the leadership of Alexander Hamilton, as the "Federalistic" party, they carried every point. This man, more than any other responsible for the misery of to-day, based all his action upon these words :

"In all civilized countries the people are *necessarily* and *naturally* divided into two classes ; the one : the few, the rich, the well-born ; the other : the many, the poor, the laboring masses." *

* This passage was quoted and approved by J. A. Garfield, the "martyred" hero of the bourgeoisie of the present day.

In 1786 deputies were sent to Annapolis to " revise " the Articles of Confederation. These articles had been agreed upon by Congress during the war and had been found sufficient to carry it through. Now the bourgeoisie claimed them as defective and insisted upon their revision, really meaning to take advantage of the opportunity and substitute for the mere federalistic compact they represented a more centralized form of government which they could use when occasion served to forward their own ends. In short, they proposed to nullify all advance gained by the producing classes in the revolution. In order to understand how far this nullification went let us examine what these classes had gained :

On the fourth day of July, 1776, the Declaration of Independence was issued. That document joined issue between England and the Colonies. When the supreme arbitrament of war rendered judgment in favor of the rebels, that judgment in effect established the Declaration as the truth, gave it the binding force of statutory law. Had those who had charge of the legislative machinery established to carry out in practice the principles whose binding force had thus been decided in theory, had those legislators so altered conditions as to enforce those principles —had they even put the principles into the new constitution, we of to-day might have been free men instead of serfs.

This Declaration announced :

" We hold these *truths* to be *self-evident :*—That *all* men are created *free* and *equal :* that they are endowed by their Creator with certain *inalienable rights :* that *amongst* these are *LIFE, LIBERTY, and the PURSUIT of HAPPINESS.* That, *to secure these* rights, governments are instituted and   .riving their *just* powers from the *consent of the governed :* that, whenever *any* form of government becomes *destructive of these ends,* it is the *right of the people* to alter or to *abolish* it, and to institute a new government, laying its foundation on such principles, and organizing its powers in such form as to *them* shall *seem most likely* to effect *their safety and happiness.*"

In other words :

1. That all men are created free.
2. That all men are created with equal rights.
3. That all men are endowed by their Creator with the right of life (and the means of living), and that of this right even they themselves cannot divest themselves.
4. That all men are endowed with the right of liberty, and that of this right even they themselves cannot divest themselves.
5. That all men are endowed with the right to the pursuit of happiness.
6. That "governments" have no other reason than to preserve these rights.
7. That whenever they fail to do so the people have a right to and should alter or abolish them.
8. That after such destruction of a false government the people have a right to establish any form of government which may *seem* to *them* most likely to give them safety and happiness.

These eight principles were the issues of the revolutionary war. The success of the rebels established these declarations as truths. Yet not one of them is to-day, either in theory or fact, the governing law of this land!

The names of the men who signed this remarkable declaration ought at least to be remembered by us. They, together with the sixteen who declined to sign the Constitution after it was formulated, comprise all of the real friends of the people among the leaders of the Revolution.

The names are these :

JOHN HANCOCK.

New Hampshire.—Josiah Bartlett, William Whipple, Matthew Thornton.

Massachusetts Bay.—Samuel Adams, John Adams, Robert Treat Paine, Elbridge Gerry.

Rhode Island.—Stephen Hopkins, William Ellery.

Connecticut.—Roger Sherman, Samuel Huntington, William Williams, Oliver Wolcott.

New York.—William Floyd, Philip Livingston, Francis Lewis, Lewis Morris.

New Jersey.—Richard Stockton, John Witherspoon, Francis Hopkinson, John Hart, Abraham Clark.

Pennsylvania.—Robert Morris, Benjamin Rush, Benjamin Franklin, John Morton, George Clymer, James Smith, George Taylor, James Wilson, George Ross.

Delaware.—Cæsar Rodney, George Read, Thomas McKean.

Maryland.—Samuel Chase, William Pacca, Thomas Stone, Charles Carroll of Carrollton.

Virginia.—George Wythe, Richard Henry Lee, Thomas Jefferson, Benjamin Harrison, Thomas Nelson, Jr., Francis Lightfoot Lee, Carter Braxton.

North Carolina.—William Hooper, Joseph Hewes, John Penn.

South Carolina.—Edward Rutledge, Thomas Heywood, Jr., Thomas Lynch, Jr., Arthur Middleton.

Georgia.—Button Gwinnett, Lyman Hall, George Walton.

The Convention finding that the bourgeoisie were represented in their body by fifty-five members and the proletariat by but sixteen, seized the opportunity boldly and sat with closed doors and in secret session. At the end of four months of terrible battle, where the heroic sixteen fought desperately but hopelessly, they brought forth the first seven articles of our present Constitution and submitted it to the States for ratification.

The sixteen who refused to sign the document were these :

ELBRIDGE GERRY, GEORGE WYTHE, CALEB STRONG, OLIVER ELLSWORTH, WILLIAM C. HOUSTON, ROBERT YATES, LUTHER MARTIN, JOHN F. MERCER, JAMES McCLURG, ALEXANDER MARTIN, WILLIAM R. DAVIE, WILLIAM PIERCE, JOAN LANSING, WILLIAM HOUSTON, GEORGE MASON, EDMUND RANDOLPH.

Then the battle was transferred from the convention to the legislatures of the various States. Though the bourgeoisie had already captured these strongholds in some of the States and had the press almost entirely upon their side, yet in many localities the proletariat made gallant struggles against it.

Jefferson wrote against it from France that it "sounded

the downfall of popular government; that its evident
tendency was aristocratic and monarchical; that it was
framed by those who are desirous of drawing over us
the substance, as they have by it the forms of the British
Government.

Hancock took the stump against it in Massachusetts
where it was only carried by a majority of nine.

Patrick Henry led the campaign against it in Virginia and denounced and assailed it with an "elo-
quence almost unrivalled." He declared "that its
adoption would be a counter-revolution more radical
than that which had separated America from Britain."
"In the warmth of debate," says Bancroft, "he seemed
even to threaten resistance if the document were adopted;
yet at last declared that even then he would remain a
peaceful citizen, only devoting his head, his hand, and
his heart to obtain redress in a constitutional (!) manner."
The measure was carried by a majority of only eight.

In New York so bitter was the opposition that notwithstanding the support of Jay, Hamilton, and Livingston, it was only carried by a majority of five.

No sooner, however, was it adopted than the storm
gathered over the heads of the aristocratic party.

So threatening was the situation that they became
alarmed and hastened to add the first ten amendments,
nine of which are for the protection of personal liberty and the tenth specifies the limit of federal powers
and guarantees all powers not delegated as belonging
to the people. Yet the major portion of these amendments have since that day been construed and legislated
out of force.

Thus much for the attempt to build a social change
peaceably upon the foundations of mere political liberty.

Space will not allow here the needed analysis of both
Constitution and Amendments. Suffice it now to say
that the former merely constituted a limited monarchy
copied after that of England, with President for King,
Senate for House of Lords, and the lower House for
that of the Commons, so called.

2

Yet the President was given more power. than the King of England had, the Senate more than the House of Lords. In the Mother-land the Lords were so by blood; here they are noble by wealth. In Britain the Commons hold their seats by virtue of their control of the soil; here the House of Representatives are seized of their seats because of their control of "votes." In both cases tyranny over and robbery of the producing classes was the only aim and is the sole result.

———

From the close of the war up to within five or ten years ago the producing classes of the Republic were comparatively well off. It is true that in all these years they were robbed right and left, but so great were the natural resources, so plentiful was the bounty of Nature, and so easy was acquisition when the land was open to all, that the robbery was hardly felt.

Blessed with the purse of Fortunatus, the worker had no desire to look too sharply after the thieves who made his pockets their own.

As the population grew in numbers the territory expanded in proportion, thus preventing, until within late years, the monopoly of lands which precedes that of labor and exchange.

In 1790 the population was 3,929,214, distributed over 239,935 square miles, the average density of settlement being 16.4 to the mile.

The following table shows the status of population to land at succeeding decades :

Year.	Population.	Territory.	Density.
1800	5,308,483	305,708	17.4
1810	7,239,881	407,945	17.7
1820	9,633,822	508,717	18.9
1830	12,866,020	632,717	20.3
1840	17,069,453	807,292	21.1
1850	23,191,876	979,249	23.7
1860	31,443,321	1,194,754	26.3
1870	38,558,371	1,272,239	30.3
1880	50,155,783	1,569,570	32.0

The rate of increase of population is so great that it is estimated that by 1890 the average density will reach 40 to the mile.

But it must be clearly understood that these figures do not by any means show that the *people* own the soil nor that there is an excess of population over and above the amount of land necessary for their support. On the contrary, they simply show that, irrespective of any other considerations, the land is more difficult of access than it ever was before and that this divorcing of the people from the soil advances in intensity in an arithmetical ratio.

This fact would be brought out with startling distinctness by a compilation of the figures showing the relative density of population on settled, semi-settled, and sparsely inhabited sections at the end of each decade, were such figures obtainable. Unfortunately they are not. But we have something at hand which serves the purpose nearly as well :

A series of maps which accompany the last census show in five degrees of density by colors (not by figures) the distribution of the population every decade.

An inspection of them shows at a glance that land is still plentiful and the population even yet far from being a crowded one ; and that the most fertile and valuable lands are the most sparsely setiled. This can mean but one thing : the holding of the good lands by monopolists either for production on a vast scale under the wage system or for speculative advance in price.

The statistics being consulted we find both to be correct ; and as well that this state of things means in plain words that the producer has been barred off of the land and the first step toward his economic slavery taken.

It is a fact much overlooked, that the geniuses of the world have sprung from the despised proletariat. And when in America a bourgeoisie developed from the producers it was not strange to find that in ability, shrewdness, and enterprise it much surpassed its class in other lands. Its colossal schemes, the daring of their execution, the magnitude of the results prove this beyond a cavil. Not surprising is it then to find that America was first in the way of invention of improved labor-saving machinery and as well perfectly competent to secure nearly if not quite a monoply of its results. No need to detail here the various inventions which have replaced the toil of man by the work of the machine, no need to particularize the various branches in which iron and steam fought against muscle and brawn and drove them from the field. The story is well known. And as well is it known how, by the control of legislative powers, the trading classes secured such legislation as enabled them to hold a monopoly of these new instruments of production and thus to add the second link in the chain welded for the perfect slavery of the workers.

One point alone remained to be looked after in order to complete the chain—the monopoly of the medium of exchange.

Of the various attempts made in the earlier years of our history to secure this monopoly, I have not here the space to deal. But the full iniquity was not perpetrated until the occurrence of the war of the Rebellion, and it will be sufficient to briefly examine that period alone.

Not content, as is their class in other lands, with the use of the money of the Government and the control over it by means of interest, here in America the bourgeoisie made a bolder stroke for power. Not content with having their own supplemental currency of drafts, bills, notes, and exchange, they aimed at and secured from the Government itself the right of issuing the government money. And with a sublimity of impudence unsurpassed in the world they made the Government pay the cost of such issue!

Having urged upon the Government a war for commercial aggrandisement against the South, the sharp Yankee traders decided in Congress assembled that the Government was unable to directly issue the money required for its prosecution. Masquerading, as representatives of the whole people, they then offered the credit of the nation for sale among the money mongerers of the world. Gold rose up to nearly three hundred

per cent. above par, and bonds fell to twenty-five per
cent. of their face value, this face value being fully one
hundred per cent. less than actual worth when we
reckon the interest subsequently paid. In plain terms,
the usurers having secured a monopoly of gold coin, by
their agents in Congress, induced the Government to
declare that this metallic medium of exchange must
serve as a basis for all other money. This created the
demand which the usurers were alone able to supply.
Of course they filled the orders at their own price,
getting as a matter of fact on money three dollars
for one, and on bonds nearly four. See the economic absurdity of the whole scheme. The usurer
says :

"The Government cannot issue paper promises to the
people. It must give them honest gold (which we
alone have). Hence it must pay us our price for our
gold." And then they take *their* price in the very
paper which they said could not be issued !

This job gave them, during the continuance of the
war, a complete monopoly of the money market. When
the war closed and no further excuses could be found
for borrowing money, the National Bank swindle, by
which the issuance of money was transferred directly to
the hands of the traders, was perpetrated. This gigan-
tic monument of impudent rascality needs only to be
hastily surveyed.

A capitalist desires to get something for nothing.
He establishes a National Bank. He has $100,000.
With this he buys $100,000 worth of bonds, goes with
them to Washington and deposits them. Upon these
bonds the Government issues to him ninety per cent.
or $90,000 in currency for circulation. Now let us see
what he can do.

With this $90,000, following out the same principle,
we will say that he buys $90,000 worth more of bonds
and deposits *them*, receiving upon them for circulation
ninety per cent. of their value, or $81,000.

He continues this process of buying bonds, depositing them, receiving ninety per cent. of their value, and
again purchasing and depositing until his capital is ex-
hausted.

The figures and amounts will be as follows :

For		Currency.
$100,000 of bonds he gets		$90,000
90,000	"	81,000
81,000	"	72,000
72,000	"	65,610
65,610	"	59,049
59,049	"	48,144
48,144	"	43,329
43,329	"	38,996
38,996	"	35,096
35,096	"	31,586
31,586	"	28,427
28,427	"	25,584
25,584	"	23,025
23,025	"	20,722
20,722	"	18,649
18,649	"	16,784
16,784	"	15,106
15,106	"	13,595
13,595	"	12,236
12,236	"	11,012
11,012	"	9,911
9,911	"	8,919
8,919	"	8,027
8,027	"	7,224
7,224	"	6,502
6,502	"	5,852
5,852	"	5,267
5,267	"	4,640
4,640	"	4,196
4,196	"	3,776
3,776	"	3,398
3,398	"	3,058
3,058	"	2,752
2,752	"	2,377
2,377	"	2,139
2,139	"	1,925
1,925	"	1,733
1,733	"	1,560
1,560	"	1,404
1,404	"	1,264
1,264	"	1,024

For		Currency.
$1,024 of bonds he gets		$922
922	"	830
830	"	747
747	"	672
672	"	605
605	"	545
545	"	491
491	"	442
442	"	398
398	"	358
358	"	322
322	"	290
290	"	261
261	"	235
235	"	212
212	"	191
191	"	172
172	"	155
155	"	140
140	"	126
126	"	113
113	"	102
102	"	92
92	"	83
83	"	75
75	"	68
68	"	61
61	"	55
55	"	50
50	"	45
45	"	41
41	"	37
37	"	33
33	"	30
30	"	27
27	"	24
24	"	22
22	"	20

$847,988, total value of the bonds on deposit at Washington.

Now he has on deposit $847,988 worth of bonds, on which for ten years he receives an *interest* of $339,195. At the end of ten years he draws out his bonds, redeems his outstanding circulation and pockets his fortune of $335,195 interest received on an original investment of $100,000 !

The reason that he don't really pursue this long-drawn-out but easy way of making a fortune, is that he can make the fortune easier and quicker in the ordinary banking business with the first capital of $90,000 which he received for his bonds.

How he does this Mr. William Harrison Riley has lately shown in these plain words:

"On every 'National Bank' note in circulation usury —'interest'— is being paid to the bankers, for not one of the notes can reach the people except through the (private) bankers, and they let none pass without usury. The manufacturers might avoid the use of taxed water, by using steam power; but they cannot avoid the use of taxed money.

"Explanation is needed of the methods by which bankers obtain more than seven or even one hundred per cent. profit per annum on their capital. I will try to explain by an illustration. To begin with, a banker deposits in the United States Treasury $100,000 in government bonds. The Government then gives him $90,000 in greenbacks, and yet undertakes to pay him three and a half per cent. interest on the deposit. Thus he will receive interest on the whole of his capital of $100,000, although he has $90,000 of the amount left at his disposal. This amount, and, say $200,000 of his depositors' money, he will soon be ready to lend. Smith borrows $2,000, on mortgage security, at five per cent. *per annum*. The *same day* he pays the money to Jones, and, before the close of the day, the money, *that was lent for a year*, is back again in the banker's safe, to be lent again the next day, at five per cent. *per annum.* Thus the banker may lend the same $1,000 bill fifty times in fifteen months, to fifty different people, and each borrower will have to pay for *a year's use* of the same money. The money that bankers lend for 'three months' or 'a year' generally returns to them in a few hours, to be lent again and again.

"The currency of the nation bears 'with it a usurer's' burden, not of five per cent. only, but of *more* than fifty per cent. per annum. For the privilege—the right—of using the 'national' currency, the people have to pay, every year, a usurer's tax amounting to *more* than half the total sum of the currency.

"If the Government will persist in paying interest on

Its bonds, then it should treat all citizens as it has hitherto treated bankers exclusively. Any citizen should be entitled to deposit bonds and receive green-backs. Thus a citizen could deposit a hundred dollar bond, continue to receive interest on it, and get ninety dollars in greenbacks, *free of interest*, when he deposited the bond. It is thus that bankers are treated. Why has the Government of this 'Republic' determined that money lenders—usurers—shall have money free of interest, and that agriculturists, manufacturers, merchants, and other workers shall not?"

A word in conclusion as to the result which must inevitably follow the future development of the competitive system in America.

The land and natural resources are being seized by corporations and capitalists, and the producer will be compelled to labor, first as a small competitor, then as a tenant, and finally as a mere wage-slave for a subsistence-wage only.

The instruments of production are daily growing more complicated, expensive, and powerful, and further removed from use by the actual producers by patent laws and legal tricks; by the power of combination and merciless competition at prices below cost, the bourgeoisie have attained and will firmly hold their grasp upon these machines; it has even now, in fact, become impossible for the workers to use them except by paying a tax which, when deducted from their earnings, leaves but the subsistence-wage.

The medium of exchange already entirely under the control of the non-producers, subject only to a tax from the Government, is already being freed from even this slight burden. By thousands of firms to-day the workmen are mainly paid in orders upon the "company-stores" instead of in cash, and upon a scheme so closely calculated as to not only leave the toiler but the barest subsistence-wage, but *as well each year to grind down his standard of living to a lower point.*

Contemporaneous with the proletariat being thus reduced to absolute slavery on the most miserable and degraded plane of existence, the operation of the system will drive the small trader out of business and into the wage-worker's ranks; it will then attack those of the bourgeoisie who have a little more and force them down in the same manner. Then the competition which has prevailed among the spoilers themselves will be replaced by combination, to fix prices of products at still higher figures.

That this combination is even now going on to a most startling extent the evidence of President Gowen, of the Reading Railroad—when he was defending that company in 1875, before a committee of the Pennsylvania Legislature, for having taken part in the combination of the coal companies to cure the evil of "too much coal" by putting up the prices and cutting down the amount of sales—conclusively shows. He pleaded that there were fifty trades in which the same thing was done. He had a list of them to show the committee, and in presenting it, this is what he had to say :

"Every pound of rope we buy for vessels or for our mines is bought at a price fixed by the committee of rope manufacturers of the United States. Every keg of nails, every package of tacks, all our screws, our wrenches and hinges, the boiler flues of our locomotives are never bought except at the price fixed by the mills that manufacture them. Iron beams for your houses or your bridges can only be had at the prices agreed upon by a combination of those that produce them. Fire bricks, gas-pipes, terra-cotta pipes for drainage, every keg of powder we buy to blast coal are purchased upon the same arrangement. Every pane of window glass in this house was bought at a scale of prices established in the same manner. White lead, galvanized sheet iron, hose, bolting and files, are bought and sold at a rate determined in the same way."

A little thought will show that all attempts to raise the wages or reduce the hours of toil of the producer are useless, since they are defeated by the inevitable rise in the prices enforced from the consumer.

Since 1875 the progress of combination has increased as does the velocity of a falling body. The inhabitants of every locality can call to mind instances so notorious as to satisfy even the most doubting mind.

These things are prophetic, because of the rapidity of their development, of the day when the people will rise in armed rebellion seeking a remedy. For pauperization entirely enslaves only when it is gradual; when it is rapid it strikes off the fetters.

When the rising—which will be one of blind, wrathful, ignorant producers—comes, then must the Socialists of America be prepared to unfurl the scarlet flag and with it in hand, head the assault as the leaders of the people, pointing out to them not only their wrongs but their only salvation : " Free land, free tools, and free money!"

BURNETTE G. HASKELL.

SAN FRANCISCO, CAL., September 1, 1884.

SOCIALISM.

CHAPTER I.

WHAT SOCIALISM REALLY IS.

WHAT is Socialism?

Should its doctrines be suppressed or propagated?

In order to decide intelligently and justly, it will be necessary to ascertain the meaning of the word "Socialism," and afterward examine its doctrines without prejudice. If, after thorough, careful, and honest investigation, it is found that these doctrines tend to degrade, impoverish, and make men unhappy, to encourage idleness, licentiousness, and crime, then the verdict of "guilty" should be found and published everywhere, the doctrines discouraged, and its disciples treated as knaves or fools. But if, on the other hand, it is proven that its doctrines have a diametrically opposite tendency, viz.: to make men wiser, better, more industrious, thrifty, honest, intelligent—to level up instead of levelling down, to raise instead of lowering the standard of manhood, to foster peace instead of war, to give liberty, equality, and fraternity to all—then should its doctrines be made known as the new and better gospel of brighter light, broader liberty and more perfect justice ; then should its disciples be encouraged and aided as the benefactors of mankind, who, possessed of a faith, proclaim it without hope of reward, and in the plainest of plain words as well.

Definition of Socialism.

Webster defined Socialism to be "a better and more just system of government."

Socialism proper is the political branch of the science

of sociology, and deals with man as a social being, his relation to society, and the methods, customs, or laws of his association, which laws and usages are summed up in the word "government." Hence, the chief province of Socialism would be to ascertain what system of government will bring the greatest amount of happiness consistent with the highest possible moral, intellectual, and physical development.

What Socialism Proposes.

Socialism proposes to abolish the system of wages-slavery, and, instead, establish governmental co-operation for production and distribution.

Socialism proposes to secure to every person who labors the full equivalent of his labor, partly in personal remuneration, and partly in social and public benefits, such as education, recreation, transportation, communication, and the best possible sustenance and care in sickness and old age—not as a charity, but as a debt that society owes to every useful citizen.

Socialism would perfect the educational system by entirely abolishing the present lack of system. The State would educate every child thoroughly, and, as they advanced, give them an opportunity to master any science, art, or mechanical pursuit for which their tastes or abilities adapted them.

Hence there would be no uncongenial pursuits or employments, as each would choose that in which he would be most likely to excel. Hence there would be very few bad mechanics, unskilled workers, or quacks at anything.

Socialism proposes scientific, intelligent, enlightened government, or free co-operation on the basis of liberty, equality, fraternity, and solidarity.

Socialism proposes to stop the wastes of society by having none of its members uselessly employed or idle, and by turning the great army of non-producers into a brotherhood of useful producers.

Socialism proposes to have more workers, and less work for each.

Socialism proposes that labor shall be a noble, healthful, and elevating duty, not an unhealthy, degrading, and slavish drudgery.

Socialism proposes that machinery shall do the world's work, and that the whole people shall own such machinery, and reap the full benefits thereof, individually and collectively, not as at present, when machinery is owned only by wealthy individuals and corporations, and operated to the degradation of the human machines who attend them.

Socialism proposes that all the natural elements and sources of wealth shall be preserved and developed by the people for the common good.

Socialism proposes that the cultivation of land is the sole title to its occupancy ; that the soil is common property, the improvements belong to the individual; that as fast as practicable and consistent with individual liberty, the government should resume title to all land, and cultivate it in large domains to the best advantage, by the most improved machinery, and the raising of only such crops as are best adapted to the soil, climate, season, etc.

Socialism advocates the doctrine that the fact of existence proves the right to life ; the right to life carries with it the right to enjoy life ; the right to enjoy life includes the highest possible enjoyment, with all the means that minister to that end, so that nothing that art or nature can produce is too good, or should be without the reach of any useful citizen who contributes his quota to the commonwealth. No food, no education, no clothes, no house or other article of necessity or luxury is too rich or costly for any useful worker, however humble in the estimation of himself or of his fellows.

Socialism advocates the destruction and utter extinction of all emperors, kings, princes, nobles, and tyrants, crowned or uncrowned, titled or untitled—no figureheads, and no castes.

Socialism advocates that the time and service of one man is equal ultimately to the time and service of any other man ; hence the nearest approach to exact justice is equal pay for equal time and expenditure of equal energy.

Socialism advocates the abolition of all war, the pacification and unification of all races and countries for mutual benefit.

Kings and capitalists make war and discord ; war and discord keep men disunited ; disunion and inharmony prevent all reform, upward tendency, and higher development.

Socialism would abolish poverty by preventing it by removing its causes. As poverty is the cause directly or indirectly of nearly all crime, therefore, by the abolition of poverty, crime would become almost unknown, and with crime would disappear all the lice, leeches, vampires, and vermin that fatten on its filth ; such as the entire legal fraternity, soldiers, police, spies, judges, sheriffs, priests, preachers, quack doctors, etc., etc.

Socialism would have money based on labor performed, and therefore represent some tangible wealth or benefit to society.

The man, therefore, who labored would have money or labor notes to the amount of service he had rendered. If he performed no useful work, he would have no money, hence no food. On the other hand, the man who had more money than he had labored for could readily be detected and deprived of that which belonged to some one else.

Under a socialistic system, extremes of poverty and wealth in the hands of individuals could not exist.

The people, in their collective capacity, would own and control all the surplus wealth of the nation or community.

Socialism Advocates Evolution and Revolution.

Socialism advocates the complete emancipation and elevation of woman to the highest plane of social, moral, and intellectual greatness which it is possible for her to attain through her own efforts and the most favorable conditions.

It advocates that she shall have equal opportunities with men to follow any profession, art, or industry, for which her education, taste, and skill may fit her ; and that for equal time and service she shall have equal honor and reward with men.

Socialism advocates evolution and revolution to accomplish the necessary and beneficent changes in our social system.

Evolution, from *e*, out, and *volvo*, to roll or unfold; hence a natural and gentle unfoldment by education from the lowest to the highest conditions of human development.

Revolution, from *re*, back, and *volvo*, to roll; hence a rolling or turning back; a turning upside down; sudden or convulsive change.

Evolution and revolution are but different phases in the same process of development.

The unfolding of a rose and the upheaval of a continent are equally natural, but while the rose imperceptibly passes through all the stages of development, from smallest bud to broadest bloom in one short season, it takes ages to mature the continent before the sudden catastrophe of an earthquake brings on the birth-pangs of the sea, and a new land is born.

Similarly, an individual or small community may become highly developed in one or a few generations, and the process may be so quiet and natural, that it is scarcely perceived; but to educate, develop, and emancipate the entire human race has taken ages of time, and almost infinite labor, and yet the process is far from being complete; so far, indeed, that comparatively few are sufficiently advanced to anticipate the impending crisis, the birth-pangs that will bring forth a new and better manhood.

Evolution is a creative, a formative, a maturing process, by easy and imperceptible stages. It is an educational, logical, and positive process, necessarily slow, but as sure as fate. Evolution is absolutely necessary to perfection and permanence, therefore we advocate it; but we believe also in revolution if the necessity arises. The shell must be broken for the weak bird. When the process of evolution is complete, every barrier must be burst, every obstacle surmounted, every impediment overcome, to establish the régime of natural justice, absolute liberty, perfect equality, even though a few individuals or cherished institutions may perish—the victims of their own prejudice and folly.

We have written thus far in a brief and general way of the objects and doctrines of Socialism, for we believe that if the American people were rightly informed on the subject, they would accept and adopt its tenets ; and such is their natural love of liberty and justice that they could scarcely wait for the necessary constitutional changes in their impatience to put its doctrines into practical operation ; but, unfortunately for the cause of truth and right, they have been misinformed on the subject, and prejudiced against it by the press, the pulpit, and politicians, who never mention it but with a sneer and to calumniate ; however, we are not surprised at this, as Socialism is the implacable foe of idleness and crime, hypocrisy, ignorance, and untruth, and without these vices to fatten on, the three " P's " would become lean indeed ; they know furthermore that, under a socialistic state, they would be compelled to do something useful and honorable for a living.

What the Three " P's " Say.

The press is the modern institution of secular knowledge, the teacher and leader in the world of intellect.

For the most part it is silent on Socialism and all phases of a reformatory and radical character. When it is forced to acknowledge the existence of Socialism, it says it is retrogressive, impractical, pulls down but never builds, divides up what is, but adds nothing to the world's wealth ; it is communistic, agrarian, a cut-purse and a cut-throat. It says that the Socialists propose to plunder those that have the good things of this life, and divide the spoils among those who have nothing ; that they intend to abolish all property, so that no one will have anything to call his own ; that they advocate such an equality that the lazy and vicious will have the same abundance and happiness as the virtuous and industrious.

The pulpit is the teacher, leader, and censor of morals, the spiritual counsellor and guide of men. It takes up the charges of the press, and reiterates them, adding its own peculiar venom, the condemnation of men and the damnation of God.

It advises the poor to be content with poverty here ; in heaven there is plenty for all. To wear the tyrant's chains on earth, and thereby earn the freedom of the skies. To submit without murmuring to injustice, insult, oppression, degradation, and even death, on the transparent fraud, that full compensation will be made in the land of the Hereafter.

Socialists are denounced as immoral, impious infidels, discontented, rebellious enemies of God and of their fellows.

Politics is supposed to be the great conservator of society, the teacher and leader in governmental and social matters. The politician knows nothing of Socialism ; but, like all ignorant and self-conceited villains, takes up and transmits the howl of the press and pulpit, adding the peculiar nastiness of his class : "They want to burst up your party." "It's a price club ; you look out for them when election time comes." "You can get all the reforms you want if you vote our ticket." "You can ameliorate your condition through politics." "Go to the primaries." "Join your ward clubs." "The Socialists are damned fools or damned thieves ; they want to divide up everything." "It is rule or ruin with them." "They have no following."

With such recommendations from the three most influential and intelligent institutions of modern times, it is no wonder that Socialism is not only misunderstood but abhorred as an unholy thing ; but the press, the pulpit, and the politician knowingly, wilfully, meanly, and maliciously misrepresent and malign Socialism ; for they know very well that if it was successful their occupations would be gone ; then the press would have no monopolists to purchase and pay it for lying ; and, as ninety per cent. of all crime would be abolished by a more equal distribution of the world's wealth, no one would keep a greasy priest in lazy luxury for the purpose of retailing stale and gauzy lies. As for the politician, the people would be too intelligent and well informed for this low thief to bamboozle them any longer.

3

CHAPTER II.

OUR FIRST REVOLUTIONARY PROPOSAL.

Abolish both the Presidency and the Senate.

ONE of the first steps to be taken is to obtain a true representative government of, by, and for all the people.

To this end all heads of governments, as now existing, must be abolished, such as emperors, kings, presidents, and governors, and with them must disappear all upper or unrepresentative houses or chambers of legislation, which were, it would seem, invented for the sole purpose of preventing popular legislation, and to impede the will of the people.

But, you ask in great dismay, would Socialists then abolish the Presidency and Senate of the United States —the two most important branches of government created by the founders of the Republic, and provided for in the Constitution?

To which we reply most emphatically: Yes; they would be among the first changes made.

The President is at best but a figure-head, more ornamental than useful; he is a king with change of name, and possesses more than kingly powers, patronage, and prerogatives.

The recent veto of the bill restricting Chinese immigration against the will of the people, as expressed through their representatives in Congress, demonstrates the dangers that threaten the destruction of a republican form of government, by the exercise of the one-man power, and reminds the people of the dangers that may, in the near future, arise to convert this Republic into the worst form of a despotic oligarchy, administered in the interest of a minority (the aristocracy of wealth) to the enslavement of the majority (the producers of wealth).

Under the present representative system no man of any party can possibly be elected President who will not submit to be bought, bullied, or cajoled by the railroads, the banks, the land-grabbers, the factory tyrants, Chinese mandarins, or the politicians.

The veto of the Chinese Bill is but one of the many acts whereby the will of the people is defied.

The President can, and does, annul the decisions of courts and juries by pardoning convicted criminals; and seldom, if ever, extending the pardoning power to protect the innocent, as was the original intention of such prerogative.

Your attention is also directed to the appointing power, whereby the President selects the heads of departments and their subordinates, numbering hundreds of thousands of voters, interested in maintaining the existing administration, however corrupt or imbecile, and also creating rings, factions, and partisan advisers, who peddle out the offices to incompetent and vicious persons, thereby producing a class of professional office-seekers. Therefore, why have a President, if he possesses the power to nullify the expressed will of the people? Hence abolish the Presidency.

The Senate is not chosen by the people, but by legislators, who are in the main corrupt tools and creatures of monopolists, who dictate their nomination and secure their election, in order to pass laws in their interest— the office of United States Senator being sold to persons having the most money to purchase a majority of votes, as has recently been the case in Nevada and other States.

As a proof that the Senate does not represent the will of the people, the vote cast on the Chinese Bill in the Senate shows that it was passed by a very small majority; while the vote in the House showed a large majority, thus demonstrating the fact that the House better understands and expresses the popular voice.

What is true of the Chinese Bill is the history of all legislation intended to benefit the masses.

The Senate should, therefore, be abolished, and the affairs of government delegated to one house of representatives, chosen directly by the people, without the intervention of party politics or corrupt nominating conventions, and without regard to State or local boundary lines.

The choice of the people should be obtained through

an improved and equitable system of representation, known as "proportional representation."

What has been said in relation to the Presidency applies with equal truth and force to Governors and State Senates; hence abolish them also.

The House of Representatives.

The House of Representatives should be what the name implies, the people's representation, and not the master, and should consist of about five hundred members, or one for every 100,000 inhabitants of the United States.

Candidates should be selected regardless of local or provincial boundary lines, and every person receiving one five-hundredths (1–500) of all the votes cast to be declared elected. Thus, suppose there are 5,000,000 qualified voters in the United States, and 500 Representatives to be chosen, each candidate receiving 10,000 votes would be entitled to be a Representative.

Referendum.

The duty of the House of Representatives would be the classification and preparation of such import laws as have been previously drafted and presented, embodying the views of any class or party upon such legislation as they may desire, and the submission of the same at stated times to a vote of the whole people for their ratification or rejection; all laws to be voted upon by sections, and should a majority of all votes cast approve of the laws submitted to them, said laws should be considered as legal and binding.

Should the people desire to repeal any law, the question should be submitted to a vote in a similar manner. This submission of all laws to the people for their approval or disapproval is what is known as the *Referendum*, a system at present prevailing in the Swiss Republic.

Imperative Mandate.

By the Imperative Mandate is meant that the representative officers or servants chosen should serve so long as they performed their duties and conformed to the instructions given them, which instructions should be imperative, and carried out in the letter and spirit; upon failure to perform the functions of office, or otherwise do as directed, the Representatives or agents should be re-called by a vote of the party whose views they were elected to represent, and others chosen by the same party to fill the vacancies, and the persons so recalled should be immediately indicted, tried, and punished with the utmost rigor if found guilty.

Special care should be exercised in electing the House of Representatives, so that not only will the whole people be represented, but also every useful trade, profession, and industry; not as at present, when the national legislature is composed almost exclusively of lawyers, bankers, capitalists, and the paid agents and attorneys of monopolists and legalized robbers generally. State and municipal governments are similarly consti-tuted, and should undergo a like regeneration.

Every citizen should take the same interest in poli-tics as he would in a joint-stock company or other busi-ness enterprise, on the success of which his well-being depended. By politics, in this connection, we mean scientific government, order, and development, not the politics of bread-and-butter scheming and wire-pulling which at present prevails.

Under the new, the higher, and the better social state, every citizen should belong to a club or organization, where all matters of public interest would be discussed, and the result of these deliberations drafted into simple laws, where any necessity existed for more law; copies could be sent to all other clubs or groups in that community or State, and laws so drafted and circulated should be submitted to a general vote once a year, and all laws receiving a majority of votes cast would be in-corporated into common law, until repealed by a two-thirds majority. Care, however, should be taken that each law dealt only with one specific subject, and, if containing more than one section, to be voted on, not as a whole, but by sections. This precaution would pre-vent the introduction of " little jokers," as the people could indorse only the beneficial, and reject the bad, without necessarily rejecting the whole.

As the law-making is done at present, nothing could be more unwise, unjust, or demoralizing.

We elect men to make laws for us.

What kind of men?

The very worst, lowest, and meanest that society can produce.

What kind of laws do they make for us?

The very opposite of what we want.

What are we going to do about it?

Under the present system, absolutely nothing, except to grin and bear it. We have no legal remedy, and we are too cowardly to apply a natural, speedy, and effective remedy, viz.: to hang every one of them. The amusing absurdity of the matter is, that not only can we not discharge them, or in any matter get rid of them, but we must pay them larger salaries than any useful mechanic gets, not for services rendered, but for the most infamous ingratitude, the grossest injustice, and the greatest injury in the power of man to inflict, viz.: to deprive us of liberty.

What beneficial society or other organization would elect a committee and pay them high wages, and then have this committee frame laws and perform acts the very opposite of that which was expected from them? What society would divorce itself from all control over committees, or a deciding vote on their acts, or would not punish or dismiss for neglect of duty on the part of any member of its committee? How much more should it punish and degrade any of its appointees who would sell the organization to its enemies, betray its secret work, slander its principles, abuse its membership, and defy its power?

No individual organization would tolerate any such proceeding on the part of its members, particularly those whom it had honored and rewarded.

But are not the interests, honor, stability, and welfare of society as a whole greater than those of any of its parts?

Is not the whole equal to the sum of all its parts?

Logically, the State is therefore entitled to the best service, the truest allegiance, the highest honor and purest patriotism that any citizen can render, and he who, having been selected to fill an office of trust or honor, fails to fulfil his duty to the State, is a traitor, a liar, and a thief—Carpenter and Humphreys for example.

From the foregoing, any person of candor and intelligence will see and admit the necessity of a radical change in our present system of government.

First.—The abolition of one-man power, the Presidency, and with it the veto.

Second.—The abolition of the Senate, an oligarchy and impediment to free government by the people.

Third.—The adoption of one legislative body by direct vote of all the people—the House of Representatives.

Fourth.—The manner of election, viz.: instead of party politics and districts, have proportional or preferential representation, whereby the largest possible number of citizens shall be directly represented by men of their own choosing.

Fifth.—The adoption of the Referendum, whereby all laws shall emanate from the people, and be referred back for adoption or rejection.

Sixth.—The Imperative Mandate, whereby all representatives, officers, agents, and servants who do not carry out the will of the people, can be immediately recalled, and others elected to fill the vacancies.

We believe that if even these few modest and conservative changes were inaugurated, that at least one-half of our present governmental iniquities would be absolutely impossible of perpetration; then monopolists would not nominate candidates whom they knew would be certain of defeat, and whom, if elected, could pass no laws in the interest of their masters, unless sanctioned by a majority of all the voters, and then it would cost too much to buy; in fact, the majority are so honest as to be unpurchasable. The people, if not hoodwinked and misled by interested and designing men, are always right, and it is an exceedingly pleasant task to record that in nearly every case where a proposition or law was submitted to a general vote of the people it received the sanction or condemnation which it deserved; as witness, the votes on the Chinese Question, the New Constitution, the San Francisco Charter, and the recent attempt to bankrupt this city with an enormous debt.

With these changes adopted, legislation in favor of capital, as against labor, would cease, and the trade of the politician and lobbyist become one of the lost arts. The exactions of monopolists from the defenceless producer, and the exploitation of labor by irresponsible capital in the hands of individuals and corporations would be at least curtailed, if not entirely destroyed.

CHAPTER III.

THE GIST OF THE NEW REPUBLIC.

Governmental Co-operation.

WE believe that the governmental and legislative changes indicated in the foregoing pages, while imperative and beneficial auxiliaries to social progress, would not alone and of themselves be sufficient to enfranchise labor from the control of capital; those are merely political and governmental changes. To complete the enfranchisement, we need entire economic emancipation, the complete bursting of the bonds, and lifting of the burdens that enchain and bow down the great mass of mankind.

In other words, we must have, instead of the present capitalistic and individualistic system of production and distribution, governmental co-operation, governmental productions and distributions; that is, that the whole people of a country, in their collective capacity, shall produce and distribute everything like a great joint-stock company, only infinitely wiser, stronger, and more competent.

Instead of the bourgeoisie system of wages-slavery for the proletarian, we must have an equal co-partnership in the world's work and wealth for the producer.

Wages is but an equivalent for a part of the thing produced; the producer must have an equivalent for the whole.

Capital is accumulated unpaid wages, or the accumulated products of labor, for which the producer received no equivalent.

If there were no profits or surplus for the employer, capitalistic production would cease, because unprofitable; profit, therefore, is the legalized robbery of labor, and the greater the profit the greater the robbery and the greater the enterprise of the robber, as the petty smuggler becomes the daring pirate, the small farmer becomes a great land-grabber, and the shopkeeper becomes a railroad king.

If the people in their collective capacity should adopt governmental production and distribution, capital, in the hands of individuals or corporations, could not compete, as the laborer would employ himself for all he was worth, and the Government, having the largest capital, the greatest number employed, and producing on the largest scale, would crush out all competition, and morally force every person into a mutual and universal alliance.

People who hear of governmental co-operation for the first time ridicule the idea that a government should find employment for everybody, and control every avenue of industry and commerce, but such people forget that either national, State, or municipal governments control or operate, in whole or in part, nearly everything else except the most vital need of society—the industrial or economic.

The national Government controls and operates the post-office; why not the telegraphs and railroads, in fact, all means of transportation and communication?

It collects the internal and external revenues, why not operate the industries on which it collects taxes?

It makes, expounds, and executes all national laws; why not prevent crime by removing its causes, by preventing poverty, by suppressing tyranny on the part of the money power and other sources of social oppression?

It maintains an army and navy in idleness and comparative luxury.

Could it not as well provide for its aged and disabled servants, and those depending upon them?

The State likewise collects taxes, makes public improvements, builds public institutions, equips its militia, and maintains a host of officials in luxury and idleness.

Could it not also go a step farther, and build houses for its citizens, schools and colleges of science, art, and industry, where all children would receive the best possible advantages of social and intellectual culture, besides a practical and theoretical knowledge in the branch of industry for which each was best adapted ?

The county and municipal governments also collect taxes, make and repair roads, streets, sewers, etc., build and maintain alms-houses, hospitals, and asylums, pay and equip a host of sheriffs, police, lawyers, doctors, clerks, and other political hacks and loafers.

Could they not just as well carry on all local industries, own all the local lands and houses, collect taxes or rents for the same, and be in every particular a genuine commune where all the inhabitants would be free, equal, and fraternal ?

Thus we see that some kind of a government controls and operates nearly every kind of an institution but the economic and industrial. It does not interfere with these because the Government is capitalistic, and to do so would interfere with the interests of private capital ; it would injure the bourgeoisie ; and they in turn would overthrow any government that trenched on their prerogatives ; to suit this class, the masses must be kept in poverty, ignorance, and crime.

The State will provide the policeman, sheriff, judge, chaplain, and even a hangman, but will do absolutely nothing to prevent the crime, but all in its power to foster and encourage wrong ; and whenever any government tries to remedy an evil, it deals with effects and leaves the cause untouched ; it dare not remove the cause, for then it would be compelled in justice to annihilate itself, for governments, as they now exist, are in their cause, operation, and end the very essence of crime, robbery, and usurpation of all natural right and natural justice.

It has often been objected, that governmental control of industries has never been tried, and is impractical.

In reply to this, we claim that the bare fact of a thing not having been tested by practical operation, is no valid or logical reason against its practicability, and certainly less against the theory on which it is based.

In the second place, we reply that governmental control of industries has been in operation in some countries, for a long time, and is to-day, in a limited sense, recognized and adopted by all.

The Government printing office at Washington is the largest printing office in the world, and turns out more and better work in a given time, at less cost, than any private institution of the kind in existence.

The post-office cannot be regarded as other than a great and necessary industry, in the success of which every citizen is interested, yet this, with all its drawbacks, Star Route scandals and defalcations, is more economically and successfully administered than any private enterprise in the country.

Again, the tobacco manufacture in France has been carried on by that Government for over one hundred and fifty years; it has reaped a large annual revenue from that industry, and supplied a better article, for lower cost, than any private manufacturer could have done; but more important even than the revenues and the cost and quality, it has on the average paid its operatives better wages than were paid to the best mechanics at any other industry, besides pensioning them after long and faithful service, and providing for widows and orphans, if any were left dependent; so well has this employment been liked, that a job in this department is much coveted and sought after, and if put on the market, would fetch a very high premium. If it is possible to secure all these successes under the worst form of modern capitalistic government, what would be the result under a socialistic form of government? We say infinitely grander, broader, and better.

Shortening the Hours of Labor.

With governmental co-operation there would be less work for each and more work for all.

If all persons able to work were usefully employed, an average of three hours per day from each would produce all the necessities and luxuries of life, with a large surplus to be added to the national or communal capital, in way of public improvements and public benefits.

Why are men compelled to work ten or more hours under the present system?

First.—Because the employer takes for his profit all over and above three hours' labor, to keep himself and other loafers in idleness and luxury.

Second.—Because men cannot get steady employment all the year round, and so are compelled to work long hours to make up for lost time.

Third.—Not more than fifty per cent. of the adult population are regularly and usefully employed. A great many labor hard at work that is useless, or absolutely injurious to society.

Shortening of the hours of labor would be the greatest boon that could be conferred upon mankind at present, for the following reasons:

First.—Suppose in the community there is a certain amount of labor to be performed in a given time, by reducing the hours of labor ten per cent., or say to nine instead of ten hours for a day's work, it follows that to complete the given work in a given time, ten per cent. more workmen must be employed; and if a legal work day was made five hours, to perform the necessary work of society, double the number of hands now employed would be needed, thus giving the classes at present compelled to be hoodlums, tramps, and loafers an opportunity to become useful members of society, besides making large drafts on those who are at present uselessly and viciously employed.

Second.—Shortening the hours of labor would give more opportunity for recreation, social and intellectual culture, and general development. The man who works long and hard cannot be healthy, educated, and refined; excessive toil brutalizes and reduces the worker to the lowest condition of animalism.

Third.—Shortening the hours of labor would speedily prepare men for other and higher reforms; in fact, we regard this measure as simply ameliorative and as a means to an end, the end being economic emancipation, and higher, nobler life.

The Wastes of Society.

In the social state, with governmental co-operation as the corner-stone, nearly all the wastes of society as now existing might be abolished.

As a people, and as individuals, we are exceedingly parsimonious in the expenditure of small amounts of coin, but yet extremely extravagant in the employment of time, labor, and material.

In the four professions of theology, law, physic, and war there are millions of the most intelligent, educated, and able-bodied men employed, for no apparent purpose but to delude, rob, and murder their fellows.

The preacher wears good clothes, eats good food, and generally lives in good houses, yet, as a preacher, he is not only worthless, but absolutely injurious, as he stands in the path of progress, opposes all reforms that he does not invent and engineer; he is always on the side of king and capital, and naturally he is their creature, and does their work. With his intelligence and education he would make an excellent teacher, did he possess a little more honesty and industry, and the churches he occupies one day in seven, would, with some slight changes, make excellent schools, lyceums, and gymnasiums for the mental, moral, and physical training of the young.

The lawyer is the most vicious and dangerous member of society; his trade is to lie, cheat, steal, and to condone and defend all crime and criminals; by instinct and training he is the friend and defender of all tyrannies, and the natural enemy of labor. Were his talents turned in a different direction he would make an excellent scientist and teacher of the higher class, in such capacity he would be a useful and honorable member of society.

The medical doctor, especially the skilful surgeon, is a necessary and honorable member of society, but the average practitioner or quack is no better than a legalized murderer; he may chop, scalp, dose, poison, and strangle you, and then give a burial permit or pass to Lone Mountain, and the law takes no cognizance of his butcheries and slow poisoning. He is a very dangerous citizen, but, under a better system, where none but those adapted by nature and education could enter the profession, might be made a very useful one.

The soldier—under this head we include not only the "regular," but all the irregulars, such as policemen, sheriffs, jailors, and hangmen. Their trade is murder— foul, premeditated, and cold-blooded. They are loafers, bummers, politicians, and dead beats; they are not only consumers, but what they cannot eat, drink, or carry away in plunder, they burn, blow up, and destroy; they lack even the saving grace of intelligence and education possessed by the other professions; their business is brutalizing, degrading, and heinous, and they follow the trade to which their instincts prompt them. Under a better social system they might be utilized as butchers, scavengers, or to do other necessary and useful labor.

These four avocations form a large part of the population of every country that produce nothing but consume the best of everything, and must be kept at the expense of the laborer, the mechanic, and the farmer. It is nearly time we had a change in this regard at least. In the support of these men, the expenditure of time, labor, and material that is wasted is enormous, appalling, and beyond belief. That number of men, with what they use and consume, might better be dumped in the ocean, and the world would be happier, wealthier, and wiser for the loss.

Another great waste of society is in the superabundance of distributors and the system of distribution.

There are at least fifty stores for every one that is necessary; in other words, there are ninety-eight per cent. more distributing depôts than there is any necessity for, and almost the same waste of time, labor, and material in the employment of clerks, porters, horses, wagons, fixtures, houses, and machinery. With governmental co-operation, all waste in the department of distribution would be abolished.

At present there is no system; every one seems to go it blind.

Twenty different milkmen leave milk to twenty different families in the same block, and these same milk-men have to drive all over the city, with great waste of time, labor, and material, to hunt their customers. The grocer, the butcher, the baker, and other distributors are compelled to do the same thing at an enormous and useless expense. Under our system there would be de-pôts of supply in every square or district, with goods of uniform excellence, free from adulteration, full weight and measure, so that there need be no choice on the part of the consumer on the score of friendship, the price, quality, or quantity, desired. Thus, at least, two-thirds of the time, labor, and operating material now necessary would be sufficient to do the same work better, cheaper, quicker, and more satisfactory in every par-ticular.

If each letter-carrier, on going to the post-office in the morning, were to fill his bag out of a heap of unas-sorted letters, and start out to deliver them all over the city to their proper addresses, it would take him a whole day to deliver fifty or one hundred letters, which he can do now in an hour or less with greater prompt-ness and certainty, to say nothing of the saving in time, labor, and material.

By proper organization, system, and discipline, a sim-ilar saving might be made in every department of dis-tribution.

A similar saving might be duplicated in every depart-ment of production, and by a proper division of labor the force now required to produce a given result could be made to yield ten times greater.

The division of labor has been very highly developed already by large manufacturers, with the best results to themselves but fraught with the direst evil to the em-ployees, of whom it makes automatons or machine-tenders. Division of labor should be introduced into every department where practical, and the saving of time, energy, and muscle should go to the producer—to the worker—not to a capitalistic loafer, who is success-ful in getting or stealing money enough to buy ma-chinery and employ slaves. All this economy in pro-duction and distribution should be utilized for the bene-fit of all, for the shortening of the hours of labor; in fact, for the abolition of labor or toil ; for the making of all happier. And here, allow me to say, that toil, hard labor—drudgery—is degrading, is dishonorable, is debasing ; loud-mouthed politicians and demagogues to the contrary notwithstanding. A horny hand is no badge of nobility, it is the mark, token, and sign of baseness ; a stooped back and halting gait, from toil, is no evidence of respectability, intelligence, and freedom, it is the visible and tangible brand of slavery. We do not despise or blame the slave ; we pity, and would teach him to be free.

CHAPTER IV.

OF THE IRON LAW OF WAGES.

GOVERNMENTAL co-operation, as treated of in the previous pages, cannot be generally adopted until the wages system is abolished ; or rather, as the wages system is gradually abolished governmental co-operation will take its place.

He who works for wages is a slave, and wages slavery is, in many respects, worse than chattel slavery.

Of course the indignant wage worker repels the charge that he, a free American citizen, is a slave.

However, it all depends upon our conception of the meaning, character, and conditions of slavery. We will name you its conditions, and then you can call it by the grandest or prettiest name you choose ; to us, the system is vile, mean, debasing, cheating, and exploiting, and we call it slavery because it fills the bill.

First.—You must work earlier, longer, and later than you wish to.

Second.—You must give closer application to your work, and perform more in a given time than you desire to or than you ought to.

Third.—Sometimes you don't want to work but must. Sometimes you want to work but can't.

Fourth.—The remuneration you receive is not a full equivalent for the labor performed, the time employed, or the thing produced.

Fifth.—A large portion of your time and labor is *directly* controlled and supervised by your employer, and the balance is indirectly supervised and regulated by the wages he pays and the system he aids in creating.

Working for wages, therefore, you are not a freeman but a slave, and a slave that your employer despises and will get along without whenever he can.

While you are young and in good working condition his avarice deprives you of many pleasures, luxuries, and even necessaries; when you are disabled, old, or sick, he will not support or care for you; in case of death he won't bury you or aid your widow and orphans, if you are unfortunate enough to have any.

In these respects you are worse off than a chattel slave.

The master sought the chattel slave; the wages slave seeks his master.

The chattel slave gave work for his food; the wages slave cannot get food for his work.

You can call this condition by what name you choose; to us it is sufficiently wretched to be called by a worse name than slavery.

The merciless economic rule under which the present system fixes the rate of wages is this, that the average wages always remain reduced to that rate which is hardly sufficient to support the life of the laborer and enable him to produce his kind; that is the fixed point around which labor always revolves, never remaining for a long time either higher or lower. Were it to remain for a long time above this point, marriages would increase, with a proportionate increase of laborers in one generation, which would again lower the standard of wages. Neither can wages, for a long time, fall below the average cost of living, as that would induce emigration and celibacy; which circumstances would decrease the number of laborers, and consequently restore the lost equilibrium.

The wages of a people are regulated by their habits of living, and these habits conform to the limits of existence and propagation.

To illustrate: In a new country, where laborers are

few and the cost of living high, wages will invariably be large in proportion ; exactly the reverse is always the case with old and thickly settled countries, as the food supply is cheaper and more abundant, with a lower standard in quality and less variety.

In China, where the country has been thousands of years settled and the population dense, the standard of living is extremely low, and consequently the wages conform to the price of rice, tea, a little fish and vegetables, which are all produced cheaply and in abundance.

In England the average standard of living among the working classes is comparatively high, and consequently wages are proportionately greater, the variety, quality, and cost of production being higher, the staples being wheat, beef, butter, cheese, beer, fruit, vegetables, etc.

In the United States, especially in California and recently developed territories, the standard of living is higher than anywhere else in the world, and here and elsewhere wages conform to the condition of existence.

A '49-er, in California, very often got $10 per day, but his meals cost $1 each and his whiskey 25 cents a drink. To-day he can buy as good a meal and better whiskey for 25 cents and 10 cents respectively, but his wages are reduced to $2, and if the average standard and cost of living continues to decrease, in twenty-five years hence his meals will cost 5 cents and his wages will be 25 cents to 50 cents, if the present wages system is not abolished in the meantime. That wages conform to the average cost and standard of living is a natural and unchangeable law, unvarying, scientific, and logical.

It is also an absolute law that the average conditions of life in a given country determine the average intelligence, morality, physical development and happiness of the people of that country ; the better the conditions of existence the better the man will be in every particular. The horse that is well bred, well fed, well stabled, well curried, and properly worked will be far superior to the animal that is badly bred, badly fed, poorly stabled, rarely cleaned, and hard worked. How long will men remain contented to be plugs and scrubs when they might change their entire condition by the desire and determination to do so ?

From the amount produced there is only so much taken and divided among the producers as will tolerably support life (wages), all over and above goes to the employer (capital).

It is, therefore, a consequence of this inexorable and cruel "Law of Wages" that the workingmen—the dis-inherited—are deprived of the enjoyment and advan-tages brought about by the progress of civilization ; for the toiler is a bare existence ; for the employer all the surplus.

Owing to increased productiveness, many articles formerly considered luxuries have reached a degree of cheapness which bring them *temporarily* within the reach of labor, and so confer a slight benefit—but, remember, *he gets this advantage as a consumer not as a producer ;* his employer has the same advantage of cheapness also, as a consumer, thus further augmenting his power to ex-ploit the consumer by an economy of capital.

But this slight and momentary advantage, which does not come to you as laborers, but as human beings, vanishes again in course of time, through this cruel and relentless law, which lowers wages to the measure of consumption necessary to a bare existence.

When the press, the pulpit, and the political economist condescend to discuss the social question, the laborer is told that he is much better off now than were his ances-tors and the workingmen of a hundred years ago.

But it must be borne in mind that production has in-creased a thousand-fold, the luxuries of life have been infinitely multiplied, and all the conditions, conveniences, and appliances that make life tolerable have been aug-mented beyond comparison with any other period of the world's history. Has the condition of the producer increased in the same ratio ? Is the laborer of to-day a thousand-fold better off than the laborer of a century ago ? We say, no !

It was stated by John Stuart Mill, in his " Political Economy," that, in spite of the enormous amount of labor-saving machinery introduced into the world, the daily toil of a single human being had not been lessened in the slightest. The startling significance of such an assertion as this will be appreciated when it is stated that, in Great Britain alone, the amount of labor-saving machinery employed is equal in power and productiveness to the combined manual labor of a collection of laborers *equal to four times the population of the entire world.*

But this is not all. Not only has the daily toil of workingmen not been lessened, but their daily remuneration, compared with the cost of living, has not appreciably increased since the introduction of labor-saving machinery. Yet the increase of wealth resulting from this enormous increase of production is almost incalculable. Where does it go? and how does it get there? are questions that are forcing themselves on the attention of society, from year to year, with growing seriousness.

Friends, the question is not—Are we better off than our ancestors? but—Are we as well off as the advanced conditions of society warrant us in being?

Are we as well off as our masters—our employers?

Are we as well off as the non-producers—the loafers and wasters of the world's wealth?

Are we as well off as we ought to be?

The answer is emphatically, No!

Then, we shall never be contented or happy until we have all that in justice belongs to us, whether it makes us happy or not.

CHAPTER V.

SOME OBJECTIONS ANSWERED.

Skilled and Unskilled Labor.

IF there is one thing more than another which disgusts the sincere social reformer, it is an aristocracy of labor. Caste or class or distinctions of honor or respectability among the useful workers of society is not only an absurdity but downright fraud and dishonesty.

The tinker and the tailor, and the butcher and the baker, and the hod-carrier and the scavenger all unite in despising and abolishing aristocratic distinctions among the wealthy loafers; they have not much respect for the difference between the Hon. Jack Ketch, the Rt. Hon. Jack Fleecem, his Excellency Jack Skinem, the

Prince of Poodledom, the Duke of Flunkeydom, the Marquis of Tweedledum, and the Squire of Tweedledee; to the honest, independent, and intelligent laborer they are all a lot of idiots and knaves that ought to be smothered in the same cesspool. So far so good. Now, friends, be consistent. Why should the watchmaker and the jeweller look down on the blacksmith, and the blacksmith on the hod-carrier, and the hod-carrier on the sand-shoveller, and the sand-shoveller on the rag-picker? just as though unskilled labor was not as useful and necessary in its place as skilled. The yearly production in the United States, derived from agriculture, was set down in 1880 at $7,500,000,000, and from manufactures $5,000,000,000. Nearly all the agricultural production was performed by unskilled labor, and also a very large proportion of the manufactures. If the farm-laborer, the hod-carrier, and the rag-picker are equally useful, why should there be any distinction of honor, respectability, or reward? This talk about skilled and unskilled labor, is a great swindle.

The man who is skilled in the chicanery of the produce market or at the mechanics' bench, is unskilled with the shovel, the pick, and the work at the transportation dock. The man who shovels on the railroad does as useful work as the engineer who runs a locomotive over it or the thief who operates the road to rob the public. If there is to be any distinction of honors and remuneration, let the man who does the most laborious and useful labor have the first distinction and highest reward.

Money.

If the present form of money is used at all, the Government only should issue it and do all banking, and money so issued should be based on labor performed. A dollar should represent one hundred minutes of time, and be called a labor note. A man doing any work would receive labor notes in pay, and these labor notes should be receivable at all Government stores and depôts for any article the purchaser might desire, equivalent to the time expended in its production to his labor note.

Under this system, where every man would get equal

pay for equal average time and energy expended, every man could have money or goods equal to the labor he had performed, and if he had more it would be evidence of fraud.

The money, or medium of exchange, should be manufactured of the most convenient, economical, and durable material to be had, and not of gold, silver, or other scarce and valuable metal. So long as the medium of exchange is gold and silver, it is liable to be monopolized by a few, who can thus enslave the many. Under the present system, an individual party can control the medium of exchange—has virtually a monopoly of the means of life in every department.

The issue of money should not be less than $100 per head of the entire population, and that amount would be sufficient to carry on all the industries of the country, and in the United States it would give us, at present, a circulating medium of about $5,000,000,000, based on the labor and wealth of the nation—the best possible basis and security that can be offered or devised.*

Interest, Usury, Rent, Profit.

Interest is the most infamous invention of man, the most cruel and unrelenting tax on labor, the cankerworm at the root of every industry, the foe of every enterprise ; it figures in the history of every crime and partakes of the essence of every evil. The murderer, the burglar, or highway robber are useful and honorable members of society compared with the usurer.

These outlaws take your money or your life at a dash and are done with it, but the interest-taker is a slow, crawling, and hideous vampire, that destroys all vigor and all bloom in life.

Is it not horrible to think that one dollar put out at compound interest for seventy years will earn more than the best mechanic can earn in the same time ? What a comment on our commercial and industrial life, that a Shylock in his den, manipulating a few thousand dollars, which he never earned, can have a dozen, a score, or a hundred producers incessantly toiling to pay him inter-

* See Appendix A.

est. Stranger still, the men so toiling and so defrauded never find fault, nay, they even defend the system that robs them, and would crucify those who point out their degradation and would help them abolish the iniquity.

Poor men often defend the system, because they take part in it by depositing their surplus earnings in bank and receiving interest thereon, little thinking that they are themselves toiling to pay that very interest, and that but for the infamous system of interest, profit, rent—usury—they could get better remuneration for half they now perform.

To illustrate : Suppose A. keeps a foundry, and B. works for him, and out of $20 per week saves $5, which he puts in the savings bank at six per cent.

A., the boss, needs funds to carry on his business, and borrows the money, at ten per cent., which B. and the other workmen have deposited at six. It necessarily follows, the employees of the foundryman must pay the interest by receiving ten per cent. less wages. If he does not take it directly from their wages, he adds it to the price of the goods he manufactures, and labor has got to pay it anyhow. But further, B. wants to rent a house, not having saved enough money to buy one. Another fellow, C., owns a lot ; he goes to the bank and borrows money to build a house, and the tenant, B., who rents it, has got to pay his interest also. If he rides on the street-cars or a railroad or steamship, to the bare and natural cost of transportation the company adds a sum sufficient to pay interest on money borrowed and large dividends on watered stock. The grocer, dry-goods man, and butcher who supply him with the necessaries of life exact from him profits sufficient to pay interest on their indebtedness and the indebtedness of the manufacturer or slaughterer from whom they purchase. The consumer, who is also the producer, has to pay every tax, interest, and profit. He has to support, either directly or indirectly, every loafer and thief in society, and for this purpose the laws, customs, and government of society garrote the laborer of 90 cents on every dollar that he earns.

We mean exactly what we say and can prove it, that cost, profit, interest, and taxes of every kind take 90 cents of every dollar that belongs to labor. We hold, and can prove, that one hour's work per day, paid at the rate of 20 cents, under the Social state, would yield as much happiness and as many of the necessaries of life to the laborer as he can now command working ten hours per day for $2. Then what a change would be wrought in his condition, working six or eight hours and receiving the full value of his production. No king could get more out of life than he, as all that nature and art could produce of use and benefit would be at his command.

Equal Pay for Equal Time and Equivalent Services.

Believing, as we do, in the democratic principle that all men are born free and equal, it follows that we should hold, as the nearest approach to absolute justice, that all men should have equal opportunities, conditions, and incentives for the achievement, of the greatest happiness and highest possible development, and, therefore, equal pay for equal time and service.

We hold that the man who prevents disease by the cleansing of sewers or other sanitary labor, is as useful a member of society as the man who cures disease after it has been contracted.

That the man who builds a house is as useful as he who designs or decorates it.

That he who makes a coat is as useful as he who sells or wears it.

That he who produces wealth is as useful as the man who protects or monopolizes it. (Perhaps a little more so.)

That he who prints a book or binds it is as useful as he who writes it.

That he who makes the canvas or makes the pigments is as useful as he who paints the picture.

Bear in mind, that if one class of men have not as much skill, education, or intelligence as the other, that they (the producers) had to support, educate, and develop the other class in comparative idleness while they were learning their professions, hence society, having conferred these opportunities and benefits on them, should have their best skill and service for the price paid to those who were all the time doing useful and active service.

In civilized society, every man is dependent upon the labor of a thousand others, and each generation is indebted for its store of material wealth, knowledge, and intelligence to every generation that has preceded it.

Independence is absolutely impossible. A self-made man is an absurdity, and a self-taught man never existed.

If you were to start off entirely naked to the woods, carrying nothing with you but a resolve to wrest from nature food and shelter, unaided and alone, even then you would be a debtor to the race for your intelligence, and to the present generation for your support until able to provide for yourself.

All useful members of society are equally useful and necessary, why, therefore, should the reward of one be so much greater than that of the other? But the climax of the absurdity is reached, when those who perform the easiest work—the least work, or no work whatever—receive the largest remuneration and the highest honors.

If all men received equal pay for equal time and equivalent expenditure of life force, each would follow that occupation for which his tastes and education best fitted him, and not, as now, the most remunerative, regardless of any adaptability or natural or acquired fitness.

As a general rule, by the present system, we have square posts in round holes, and round posts in square holes.

Under the Social state all schools, colleges, institutions of art and mechanics would be open and free to every citizen, regardless of age, color, class, or condition, and the best possible facilities afforded each person to acquire a thorough theoretical and practical knowledge of any trade or profession he might select, without any pecuniary or other expense to either himself, his parents or friends; then he would not have an excuse to charge compound interest on the outlay for his education and profession—claiming that he had spent so much time and money, besides undergoing various privations, hardships, and self-denial to acquire a lucrative and respectable calling, and that, having incurred all this, he was justified in charging more for his services than a hod-carrier or a sand-shoveller.

Why should the surgeon charge $100 for cutting off the leg of a mechanic, while the same mechanic, for making the instrument the surgeon used, got only two or three dollars per day for an expenditure of ten times the time and muscular energy, with one-fiftieth of the pay that the doctor received?

Again, why should he charge the printer, the book-binder, the schoolmaster the same amount, when without their services he could not have learned his profession? Again—the mechanic could not have made the instruments, or the printer, bookbinder, or teacher done their share but for the coal and iron miner, the farmer, the tanner, the miller, the butcher, the cook, etc.

Even among the hardest and most useful workers there is caste and an aristocracy of labor.

The mechanic thinks himself a superior being to a hod-carrier or shoveller, and the insignificant thing behind a counter puts on airs over both the mechanic and laborer.

Back of all and above all stands the capitalist who filches from all and says: "But for *me*, but for *my* money, but for *my* enterprise, *my* brains, *my* pluck, none of you would have anything; *I* employ you all; *I* feed, clothe, and house you all." When the real truth of the matter is that it takes every one of us—laborers, mechanics, clerks, and professional men—to keep one capitalist. It takes all our time, brains, energy, and industry to keep the loafers of the world in luxury and idleness. A thousand men must sow in toil and tears that one may reap in gladness. A thousand babes go supperless to bed that one monster brat may puke on silk.

A thousand factory girls drudge out their weary lives in stint and squalor that one factory lord may coin their blood and bones and brains to deck the mistress of his lust and ease.

A hundred thousand railroad men must sweat and toil and suffer the whole year that one low brute may spread a banquet for his kind.

And wherefore should it be thus?

Wherefore, but because knowledge is power and ignorance is weakness.

Our oppressors are stronger because they know more, and we are weak because we are ignorant—ignorant of our rights, ignorant of our duties to ourselves and to society, ignorant of the objects and methods of organization, ignorant of scientific government, but, above all and worst of all, *we are densely and stupidly* ignorant of our own ignorance.

But it is consoling that in life we shall never know less, and the probabilities are that we shall know a great deal more before long.

Some of our fellow-laborers have been to school, and the rest of us have met the scholars, and the scholars, with all the enthusiasm and impetuosity of youthful learners, have been telling us the wonderful things they have been taught, and we have listened attentively, with eyes wide open and mouth agape, and have resolved to attend school ourselves and tell all we know to our comrades, who cannot attend, or do not care to learn.

Equality of Woman.

Socialism was the first, and is still, the only political, social, or religious organization which recognizes the perfect equality of woman with man.

It is true there are at present organizations not socialistic which advocate " Woman's Rights "—that is, their right to vote and scramble in the mire of politics for political office, their right to make idiots and knaves of themselves, their right to join with the priest and the politician in completing the enslavement and utter degradation of themselves and the man also. With that class of long-haired, mush-headed, sentimental idiots we have no affiliation or sympathy.

The ballot, under the present system, is a "delusion and a snare ;" it has debauched, enslaved, and degraded man ; it would do the same for woman, but in a greater degree, as the cleaner and purer the person or thing is, the more easily defiled and the more filthy appears the defilement.

If the ballot or universal suffrage had any inherent virtue to abolish injustice and tyranny and to establish justice and liberty, our masters would never have armed us with such a deadly weapon; they know well that they were arming children and idiots with toy pistols and rusty sabres to strut around on Fourths of July and election days, aping the deportment and actions of firemen and philosophers. And, furthermore, they knew that if the idiots ever attempted to organize and use their rusty sabres in dead earnest, it would be a simple matter to divide, discomfort, and disarm them.

Nay, gentlemen, some of us are not children or idiots any longer; when the crash of panic and revolution spreads over the land we shall want Gatling guns and dynamite, instead of more toy pistols and rusty sabres for our sisters to play and dirty themselves with.

Under the present system, the press, the pulpit, and the politician control ninety per cent. of the male vote; the female vote would be controlled in a greater degree by the same influences, especially that of the church.

We do advocate that the conditions and opportunities for betterment shall be the same for woman as for man; that she shall receive equal remuneration for equal time and service; that every trade, profession, and occupation shall be open to her, and no other impediment or conditions imposed than those that are placed upon man, viz.: her *fitness*.

Woman must be made financially free and independent of man.

Until her financial emancipation is achieved, she will be the slave of man. If woman was financially free, she could marry when, where, and whom she pleased.

She could then marry for love, and not for a living, as now.

She could then marry a man who loved her, and not a brute to enslave her.

Woman should be the equal comrade, companion, competitor, and helpmeet of man through all the honorable toil and battle, leisure and pleasure of life.

When man has demonstrated his fitness to use the ballot aright, woman should wield it too; not before.

Adulteration of Food.

It is a self-evident proposition that without abundance of wholesome food, comfortable clothing, large, clean, well-ventilated workshops and dwellings, together with the best hygienic and sanitary conditions, in individual and social life, it is impossible to have a healthy, happy, and well-developed race of men.

Therefore we believe that in those respects we could approach nearest to perfection under a system of governmental co-operation, as by it the entire infamous practice of adulteration would be abolished. The people in their collective capacity would produce only the best and purest of everything needed for use or consumption, there being no incentive or compulsion, from profit or competition, to adulterate, cheat in weight or measure, or otherwise misrepresent.

At present nearly every article we eat or drink is adulterated, and generally with injurious substances that act as a slow but certain poison.

Who consumes adulterated food and drink? The rich? No. They have money enough to buy the purest goods in the largest quantities, so that wealth has not only the advantage of quality but also the advantage of cheapness.

The poor man is compelled, through his poverty, to purchase the coarsest and most impure goods in the smallest quantities, thus having the three-fold disadvantage of small quantity, bad quality, and dearness.

The poor man is the helpless victim of every adverse condition and the defenceless prey of every social shark, from the cheap hash-house and grocery keeper up to the giant railroad robber and mammoth land thief.

Under governmental co-operation, all dwellings, workshops, towns, and cities, would be built in the healthiest locations on the most scientific principles, with a view to securing the best possible sanitary conditions, and the largest, healthiest, and happiest life for all.

Benevolent Societies.

Benevolent, insurance, and secret societies are a comparatively modern institution, nearly all of them having been devised and developed within the last fifty years; but society at large is now so honeycombed with them, that the man who does not belong to one or more is a curiosity and a friendless waif; as much alone in the city crowd, and church, and tumult, as if he lived in a wilderness.

Let us briefly investigate the philosophy of their cause and growth. Shakespeare says, " Man looks before and after," in contradistinction to the lower animals, that remember but little of yesterday and take no thought for to-morrow.

Man is peculiarly a social animal. He associates, first, because it is nature to do so? second, because it is his interest to do so for self-protection, support, and companionship. Increased facilities of communication and transportation have, as it were, concentrated, introduced, massed, and centralized mankind, which, together with the press, the increase of commerce, education, and general intelligence, have made the possibilities of organization almost perfect.

The decay of feudalism and the kingly power and the growth of democratic ideas have had a tendency to destroy nominal inequalities and unite hitherto sundered interests and classes.

But the bourgeoisie or money power, the trading-class, the merchant, employer, and monopolist taking the place of absolute monarchy and feudalism, gradually assumed all the powers and prerogatives of tyranny, thereby compelling the proletarian to unite in self-defence.

It is a fact well worth noting that ninety per cent. of all secret, benevolent, and insurance societies belong to the so-called " lower " and " middle " classes of society, such as laborers, mechanics, and small traders or business men and poor professionals. When they amass wealth sufficient to be ranked with the upper classes, they either withdraw directly or drop out gradually from all such organizations, having no further use for them or need of them. The necessity for continuing in benevolent societies ceases to exist.

There are some notable exceptions, however, who do not withdraw—these are the politicians, the office-seeker, the ambitious demagogue. Such men can always have use for a secret organization to further their ends.

There is but one secret organization in which the majority of the membership is wealthy, and where if poor men enter they never rise to any prominence, no matter how intelligent or honest, unless they amass large wealth or wield great political power. It is composed chiefly of the governing classes and the upper bourgeoisie—the natural enemies of labor. This not being, strictly speaking, a benevolent society, but an association of aristocrats, for mutual admiration and aggrandizement, we shall pass it without further comment.

The objects, avowed or implied, of secret and benevolent societies is to protect the poor and weak against the rich, strong, and unscrupulous. To provide for a rainy day.

The poor man, by promising to do the same for others of his kind, insures to himself and his family, in case of sickness or accident, a small allowance to procure the necessaries of life, and, in case of death, a decent burial and in some instances a bonus to secure the surviving dependents from immediate starvation.

In making this partial and uncertain provision, the poor man, with little knowledge of the social question, almost totally ignorant of his worth and his rights, and of the duties of society, has builded as well as he knew how—as well as the circumstances would permit; in fact, as well as he dared to build ; for had he gone to bedrock and laid his foundations broad and deep, and attempted to rear his structure proud and strong, he would have been defeated at the outset by the bourgeoisie—the governing class, the money power ; for these tyrants very well know that as labor becomes intelligent, united, and aggressive, their power, influence, and wealth decrease in the same ratio.

Under the Social state there would be no need of benevolent societies, as it would be the duty of the state to provide for all who were unable, from any cause, to provide for themselves.

A man can produce in ten years, from the age of twenty to thirty, working six hours per day six days in the week, more than he can consume without wasting in a lifetime of seventy years.

By natural right, therefore, the State should hold in trust for him his surplus produce, to be drawn on at any time the necessity arose, and also to be utilized in educating and training others to become intelligent and useful citizens. In thus providing for all, out of their own, the state bestows no charity, and the recipient incurs no obligation and loses no independence or self-respect, any more than if he had personally hoarded his surplus earnings and utilized it to his advantage in case of need.

Hoarding, saving, squeezing, so as to make provision for the future is one of the most degrading phases of human endeavor, and the prolific parent of a thousand forms of crime, to say nothing of its baneful effects on social life and national character.

Socialism in this regard would make the individual superior to his fate, superior to the conditions that thwart and wreck solitary effort in the achievement of security and independence.

Bees hive no honey where perennial flowers abound, and if a wandering swarm from frigid climes, seeking should find those southward fields where fruit and blossom blush and bloom together on one fragrant bough the whole year through, their thrifty instincts for awhile would hoard the teeming nectar of exhaustless sweets, but when experience taught that summer never went or winter came, they would cease providing for a stormy time, and change laborious days for joyous ease, the miser's scantiness and care for generous life and free.

Man by association and universal corporation could abolish the rainy day, the winter time in every individual life, and relieve him of the necessity of stinting, starving, and pinching himself to make a small and uncertain provision for the evil day by inventing, fostering, and supporting benevolent societies based on the capitalistic idea and radically wrong ; narrow, prejudiced, bigoted, incompetent, and idiotic in their conception and operation. They are capitalistic, because every man before joining must be a capitalist to some extent; he must have means to pay initiation, dues, and assessments, however small.

They are narrow and conservative, because there are certain qualifications of faith, race, nationality, or morality required of those who would join.

They are unjust, because no matter how much a man may have paid in, or how hard he worked for the good of the order, or how much in need of assistance, if he break certain arbitrary laws, he is debarred from all benefits, they take his money, time, and labor, and give nothing in return—nay, worse, if he incurs great displeasure by any breach of faith, they blackmail him, and hound him down until death delivers him from their accursed clutches; in some cases they even go so far as to inflict the death penalty, which in our opinion is more cruel and inhuman than their system of espionage and blackmail.

We need a benevolent society, but it should be one of universal good, where each member draws benefits from the cradle to the grave. We need a Universal Brotherhood, based on Liberty, Equality, Fraternity, and Solidarity.

Those who believe in and belong to secret and benevolent societies are like

> " A child that's crying in the night,
> A child that's crying for the light,
> And with no language but a cry."

They are groping in the darkness; instinctively they feel the necessity of light and know it exists, but cannot find it, or finding it burn their fingers in its flame. We need organization, but not mystery, darkness, and humbuggery. We need benevolence, but it should not be contracted or sectional, but broad enough to embrace all mankind, and minister to every necessity; not as a charity, not as a lottery; not as a gamble, not as a swindle, but as a duty, as a right which the collectivity owes to the individual, in return for the benefits conferred on the collectivity by his existence, passive and active usefulness.

5

CHAPTER VI.

OF THE MEANS TO THE END.

Trades-Unions and Strikes.

TRADES-UNIONS and strikes are valuable as a means to an end, the means being education, the end emancipation.

An ignorant Socialist may despise and denounce the trades-union, but in it the social philosopher sees an absolutely necessary stage of development in the social evolution of man. In the life of Labor, trades-unionism is the schoolmaster (the pedagogue) who brings labor to the feet of the great teacher (Socialism) for higher, broader, and better instruction.

The union gives practical object-lessons in organization, in self-reliance, in independence; it has dissected and analyzed the boss, the master, the employer, and now the laborer no longer uncovers his head and bends his knee in the presence of the petty tyrant; he no longer treats him with the obsequious respect and deference of other and more ignorant days. In dissecting the carcass of the capitalist he found it rotten, and now he holds his nose when it passes by.

The man who says that no good ever comes of strikes proclaims himself an ass. There never was a strike, however "unsuccessful," that was not morally worth millions, not only to those immediately interested, but to the remotest toiler on the world's wide rim. In fact, there never was an unsuccessful strike in the history of labor, and, furthermore, the most unsuccessful strike, so far as increased remuneration was concerned, has been in the end the most beneficial for labor generally. It resulted in strengthening determination and resistance, in reinforcing organization, in rectifying mistakes, and avoiding the former causes of failure. Above all, and best of all, it showed them the utter heartlessness and greed of capital. It showed them that capital (in the hands of individuals) and labor are not, and never can or will be, friends, however much the editor and preacher may prate and argue to the contrary.

Yes, we hail the Union and the Strike as our best auxiliaries in the battle for economic freedom ; but the striker is going it blind ; he knows, he feels there is a social disease, but is utterly ignorant of its cause and costs. He must learn, he will learn in the near future, that the sole cause of his trouble, of the trouble, misery, and destitution of the proletarian everywhere, is not in the employer, the capitalist, but in the power behind the capitalist, that power which, created, still sustains and protects him in his crimes against labor, viz. : the *Government ;* and the remedy is to abolish all government, as now understood, substituting in its place, not a RULER, but a simple administrative machine by which we as the people can do our own business. Thus you destroy the entire system of slavery, and thus *only* establish perfect LIBERTY.

Political Action.

In several European countries where the elective franchise is conferred on those who possess property qualifications, and known to be naturally conservative, it is thought by labor reformers in such countries that universal suffrage is the true panacea for all social and political evils, and hence they waste much time agitating for this ameliorative measure, forgetting all the while that if the ballot was the potent factor it is claimed to be, that if it could right all wrongs, abolish injustice and tyranny and establish Liberty, with all the good obtainable--that such a two-edged sword, such a magic staff, would never be placed in the hands of labor by any government in the world, for the very logical reason that it would be suicidal, as the greatest of all evils is capitalistic government ; and if the ballot had any beneficent power and wisdom, it would first of all be directed against government, as the fountain, source, root, and origin of all tyranny and injustice.

In the United States we have had universal, or rather manhood, suffrage for over one hundred years, yet the condition of the producer, the proletarian, is not one whit better through the exercise of the ballot than his fellow-slave of Russia, Germany, or England; if he is, socially, financially, or in any respect, better fixed than his European brother, it is owing to other conditions, of population, expanse of territory, resources, and other natural conditions entirely independent and exclusive of political or social life; hence we have long since arrived at the conclusion that the ballot is a failure, a delusion, and a snare; that through it the present system can never be abolished or any large and permanent good obtained. We are, therefore, opposed to political action—for the following reasons, also:

First.—IGNORANCE. Labor is ignorant of its rights and duties, ignorant of the causes of social wrongs, and the proper remedies to apply. Labor is either uneducated or wrongly educated on economic questions, and all matters of vital importance in social science.

Second.—SLAVERY. The individual or corporation that employs a number of workers virtually owns and controls their persons and functions; hence their votes. To vote rightly means to vote against the interest of the employer: result, starvation to the man who has the bravery to do right.

Third.—CORRUPTION, the result of poverty and exfoliation. A man sells his vote because he needs the price of it; if he got the full result of his labor, he would not be under the necessity of selling his liberty to buy bread. Thus the system produces poverty, and poverty reproduces and perpetuates the system; but eventually in Sociology, as in animal procreation, breeding in and in will produce degeneracy, decay, and death, and tyranny and poverty will go out together forever.

Fourth.—DEMAGOGY. Party politics, religion, nationality, and side issues are used to divide labor and prevent it voting and acting in its own interest.

Fifth.—LAW. The entire Government which is engaged in making, expounding, and executing laws for the spoliation of labor and the aggrandisement and protection of the bourgeoisie is capitalistic in every country; and if, by accident, labor for awhile should be united and have passed beneficent laws, the judges would declare every one of them unconstitutional and inoperative. So long as capital owns the judges, the soldiers, the police, the prisons and forts, labor may vote as long and as often as it pleases, and no good will result; hence we do not believe in or advocate political action under the present system.

How then do you propose to effect the desired change?

By educational methods only, until a large majority or an intelligent minority are convinced that the present system should be destroyed and a better substituted. Being thus prepared to make the change through force of numbers and intelligence, if opposed seriously by capital and those whom it could hire to do its .fighting, we would adopt *Revolution* to the extent of the utter extermination of idlers, robbers, and tyrants.

Agitation! Education!! Organization!!!

With these three weapons we propose making both a defensive and aggressive warfare on all forms of social iniquity. These words, and the things they signify, shall be our arms and armor, our shibboleth, our sword and shield.

Agitation means stirring up, shaking—it might be called the friction of fluids. We propose to stir men up, to shake them out of the lethargy of despair, the sleep of ignorance and intellectual death. We propose a friction and chafing of men's minds until a healthy action is produced.

We propose to make men dissatisfied with their lot, discontented with their conditions, as we know well for the dissatisfied only is there hope of highest achievement, and discontent is ever the prophet of progress.

But for the continual agitation and mutation of the physical world, death and chaos would be the immediate result. Content and quietude are incompatible with life and progress.

But for the winds and waves and tides and currents of the ocean it would become a stagnant pool of filth and slime, disease and death, resulting in the speedy extinction of all animal and vegetable life on the planet. Similarly, but for the continual agitation in the intellectual and social life of man, he would long since have become extinct as a rational and progressive being.

Frail barks sometimes go down at sea, and mighty ships are wrecked by mightier winds, and well-built cities swept by tidal waves, and in the bark, the ship, the town, some good and pure may meet untimely death ; but for every victim nature blindly bleeds, ten thousand better lives are blest.

The wind that wrecked the ship may carry freight of golden showers to bless a continent with bloom and fruit, and in its rapid flights to further seas that self-same wind may be the scavenger of eastern plagues, and bear the pestilence from torrid climes to frigid shores. So, too, the social agitation may wreck frail institutions, and bury bonded wrongs, having no re-spect or mercy for those who choose to perish for their prejudices, traditions, and superstitions ; but the real, solid, and material good conferred on man will infinitely outweigh the apparent evil and temporary disturbance of social conditions. Remember this, the whole is greater than any of its parts, and, *à fortiori*, the well-being of the whole race paramount to the well-being of its smallest and most vicious complement. The whole race must be enfranchised, purified, and elevated to the highest attainable ultimate, regardless of suffering to individuals or disaster to cherished iniquities.

Educate. This means a gradual unfolding, develop-ment, evolution of the mind.

When we speak of education, we do not mean to cram with odds and ends of book knowledge, as they do in schools and colleges. We mean what the word literally signifies, to lead out, to unfold, to develop the mind, to make men think, and, more important still, to make them think rightly, rationally, logically—to make them understand their rights, and how the greatest happiness can be obtained, not alone for the greatest number, but for ALL, without regard to race, color, and condition, time or place.

Knowledge is power ; therefore ignorance is weak-ness, and Socialism cannot wield or mould a mass of ignorant men, and persuade or force them to do what is right and best for themselves. They must first be edu-cated, then all the rest is plain sailing.

If you could persuade or force ignorant men into a

certain groove to-day and to-morrow withdraw the
moral suasion or the force, or that stronger influences
should be used to swerve them from the right, all your
labor would have been wasted, unless the understand-
ing is first captured. Even if we had the power to *force*
men into our way of thinking, it would be tyranny to
exercise it—the very thing we are trying to combat in
every shape ; besides, tyranny is always morally weak,
and the oppressed vigilant for an opportunity to revolt,
and what is gained by the sword must be held by the
sword ; what one revolution by forceful methods obtains, a more perfect revolt of arms can wrest from the
recent despoilers. Education, therefore, must precede
and prepare the way for successful permanent Revolution.

Organize—which means to combine or associate in
harmony, to amalgamate, to form a homogeneous mass,
to assemble in complete order and detail, as a body
which is an assemblage of organs, each with its exclusive, proper, and necessary functions. A jumble of
heads, legs, tails, eyes, ears, stomachs, entrails, etc., no
matter how many, would never constitute a body; in
fact, the more of them there were without the spirit of
organization, the more corrupt and unwieldy would be
the mass of putrefaction.

In the world to-day there is more discontent and dis-
satisfaction with existing conditions than in any prior
period of its history.

And, although the masses have not yet begun to be
educated, yet with the materials of discontent and oppression on hand, to start with, great changes in the
social system could soon be wrought if there was any
harmonious and concerted action on the part of the
producers, the exploited, the proletarians, the Adullam-
ites of society. Organization would facilitate education, and precipitate the revolution, if one should be
found necessary. But organization of the right kind is
the chief difficulty that we have to overcome.

Some of the chief difficulties in the way of organization, and the remedy for them, are as follows :

First.—Ignorance as to the evils of the present system, and the true methods of eradication. General

discussion, agitation, and education through public meetings, the Labor press, and Labor literature will aid materially in allaying this trouble.

Second.—Differences of race, religion, language, and industrial pursuit are used by the bourgeoisie to keep the proletarians of the world divided and antagonistic. A more general diffusion of knowledge, the obliteration of national boundaries, the bursting of traditional barriers, art, science, communication, transportation, a more general intercourse and better acquaintance of the world's workers will result in teaching them that the cause of labor is the same the world over, and that their masters magnify fictitious differences to keep them from uniting to obtain their rights.

Third.—Suspicion and distrust of leaders, the masses having been duped and betrayed so often, have but little faith in reformers and their manners of relief. The quick, certain, and ignominious " taking off " of all traitors will cure this cause of disunity.

Fourth.—Internal dissensions caused by sore-heads and would-be leaders. Abolition of all personal leadership, and imposing the most laborious and dangerous duties on the most prominent and ambitious will have a tendency to check, or at least to try and prove the moral courage and physical daring of all aspirants for the honors of *immolation.*

Fifth.—Internal dissensions, caused by the paid agents of capital and the governing class to defeat the objects of labor organizations and retain in their own hands all wealth, authority, and honors.

Quick, certain, and ignominious death to both agents and principals will have a very salutary effect in this disease, if applied on the first symptoms being discovered.

LACK OF INTEREST.—Workingmen take very little interest in organizations to ameliorate their condition. (*a*) Because they look for immediate, tangible results, each for himself individually, and failing to receive any, quit in disgust. (*b*) Lack of time to attend meetings, being worked too long and too hard. (*c*) Inability to pay dues, fines, assessments, etc. (*a*) The business carried on is generally of a stale and routine character, often

frivolous and even acrimonious. Besides, teach men
that they must not depend on their fellow-slaves for
work, bread, or burial. They should exact that much at
least from the robber that exploits them. Fight for
shorter hours of labor first, and increased pay must logically follow; but abolish, as far as practical, all dues,
fines, etc., make the meetings as interesting as possible; offer inducements to the younger and more retir-
ing members to give their views on the subject in debate.
Encourage the *esprit de corps,* not for the purpose of
rivalry among different branches of labor, but to encourage the spirit of fraternity and solidarity among the
useful workers of the world.

Possible Practical and Final Action.

When the Social question, called also the Labor question, has been thoroughly agitated and understood; when
the masses are educated in their inherent and natural
rights, and are ready to not only demand them but to
enter into their full, free, and permanent possession, and
when the great mass of producers in any country are
thoroughly organized, locally and generally, in groups,
clubs, and assemblies—then, and not until then, should
the local or district organizations hold a general election
to send delegates to a national convention or general
assembly.

Each delegate elected should be thoroughly educated
on human rights of labor, and the necessity of an immediate and thorough change in the existing social
system.

This general assembly should meet openly in a central
location, entirely untrammelled by fear, favor, or prejudice, and then and there carry out the spirit of their
instructions and teachings by drafting a general constitution or bill of rights, based on principles of natural
law, liberty, justice, and pure reason.

This bill of rights should then be submitted to the
whole people for a general vote in their local organizations, and if adopted by two-thirds of all such clubs,

with not less than two-thirds of the entire numerical vote of the country; it should become the fundamental law of that country, and provision made to put it in full force immediately.

If, however, its operation met with opposition from the non-producers, the capitalistic loafers, robbers, and the governing class, it would be in order for the people to execute their will regardless of whom it hurt, what superstition was crushed or prejudice assailed.

In such cases force might be necessary; so it is sometimes expedient to amputate a putrefying limb to save the body from death. But we believe that if a large majority of the people of the country was sufficiently educated on those questions as to put them into practical operation, they would meet with very little opposition from the ignorant, vicious, and interested minority; and even the small prejudice against the new order of things would soon expire under the benign influence of liberty and justice, for it requires but a small amount of acumen to perceive that under such a system as we propose the bourgeois, the capitalist, the king, the loafer, and the titled robber of the present day, shorn of all their honors, privileges, and prerogatives, would be infinitely better off than they are now. As a useful citizen each could have and enjoy, without remorse for the past and any fear for the future, all the benefits of the highest civilization, all that nature and art could contribute to make men happy — what more has he now?

Nay, less. For each carries in his breast the uneasy consciousness of guilt, the knowledge of unnumbered wrongs, the hideous memories of murders foul, and black remorse for unconvicted, unforgiven crimes.

However, our concern is not for the oppressor. We are not particularly stuck after making tyrants happy; our object is to elevate and make happy the deserving, and finally make all deserving, even the king.

This is what within the bounds of possibility may occur, but it is by no means the probable outcome of the present lamentable state of affairs. What will be far more likely to happen is this:

Probable Course of Future Events.

A careful study of the present competitive system of industry, since the introduction of machinery, and the consequent enormous increase in the productive forces of the world, shows this:

That by reason of the entire want of system which characterizes mere profit production, upon the slightest demand, goods of every character are thrown upon the market in quantities far exceeding the purchasing capacity of the consumers. That this same profit production, in its heartless competition to produce cheaper goods and thus secure a sale, acts continually to reduce, to the lowest possible point, the wages of the producer; that since this producer is at the same time the consumer it follows naturally that the more he produces the less he produces for, and the less he is able to purchase or consume. Hence capitalistic production is busily engaged in cutting its own throat.

The result of this continuous suicide finds expression in certain social convulsions denominated "panics." These are the result of capitalistic production and of that alone. Enormous quantities of goods are produced, and produced so cheaply that the producers (laboring for a mere subsistence wage) have no money to buy them. Unable to dispose of their goods a wave of bankruptcy overwhelms the employing class; manufacturers and dealers alike are ruined; factories and stores are closed; thousands of workers are thrown idle and hungry upon the streets; they revolt, perhaps, as they did in 1877, and as they will in 1884; the military power is invoked, the workers are shot down, the pressure upon the labor market is removed; then the surplus stock of goods is gradually absorbed; production starts up again, feebly at first but afterward with renewed vigor and strength; and so the game goes on, to be played again and yet again.

But careful observers, studying these facts, see that each panic increases in intensity and that its desolating effects widen in ever-increasing circles. They foresee that within the lifetime of the present generation the final climax will come when millions of starving workers will raise in our streets the old, dread cry for bread or blood. They foresee that these men will be desperate, ignorant, and bloodthirsty, aiming at chaos instead of order.

We who see this, the Socialists, would prevent it; not by preventing the revolution, for that is impossible, but by guiding and controlling it, so that its ultimate result will be perpetual peace on earth, good-will to men.

In this book, which necessarily is but fragmentary, we have used the English language in the plainest and bluntest manner. Writing for workingmen we have written so that they might understand.

It is fit in closing that in one brief paragraph we should lay down the scientific formula upon which our movement is based :

The cause of misery, crime, and unhappiness among the producers of the world is mainly due to the monopolization by a class of non-producers of the land and the natural resources of earth, the tools and machinery of production and the mediums of exchange, communication, and transportation. To abolish this cause and remedy these evils the abolition of private property in the things mentioned is the first necessity ; the next is their seizure for common use for the collective benefit of the producing community.

That this is a truthful statement no wise man will dare to challenge. That within our lifetimes all men shall see it so, the coming years will prove.

S. ROBERT WILSON.
A. J. STARKWEATHER.

SAN FRANCISCO, CAL., September 20, 1884.

APPENDIX A.

SUPPLEMENTAL CHAPTER.

On the True Basis of Value and Money.

(Note to page 54.)

THE most important doctrine of Socialism is that relating to money. The only reason for the existence of any circulating medium is to facilitate the exchange of commodities. The loafers of the world, unwilling or unable to produce any of the necessaries of existence, and thereby honestly earn their living, have devoted their most subtle arts and employed their most cunning schemes in the trade in, and monopolization of, the means devised by them to exchange the goods of one producer for those produced by another.

In strict justice, this exchange of the value produced by one with another should be equal—that is to say, the goods produced by the farmer should be exchanged for goods of *equal value* produced by the mechanic. Were this the case the loafers of the world would either have to work or starve. But under the present ingenious and impudent system, Mr. Loafer, under the pretences of "distributing the produce of labor," or " providing the medium of exchange," and by means of such infamies as " rent," " interest," " profit," etc., stands between the toiling and idiotic producers, and, before their eyes, under the highwayman's mask of " law," and with the pistol of the Competitive System, coolly filches from them all that they produce over and above that amount necessary to enable them to continue their unavailing toil.

The whole present system of money must be totally destroyed. A dollar now has no basis of value ; to-day it may represent fifty pounds of flour, a month hence, only twenty-five pounds ; to-day it represents twelve hours labor of a Chinaman, nine hours labor of a white man, twenty-four hours labor of a white child, and thirty seconds loafing of a Vanderbilt. (I hope not also to forget that it is the street price now paid by some loafer's whelp to the workingman's daughter who is compelled to sell her body for bread.)

Socialists, who have thought deeply upon this proposition, truly claim that we must have some FIXED standard of value whereon to base the exchange of commodities. This standard must not be an arbitrary one, but must be CREATED by natural law and discovered by Science.

A producer can only claim compensation for what he produces, upon the proposition that he is entitled to receive in return for what he has produced that which he has expended in its production. In other words, cost must be the limit of price. In the production of any specified article the laborer self-evidently expends but two things, first, his time, and second, his life-force or energy. It is as self-evident that the TIME occupied by one worker is equivalent to a similar period of time devoted by another ; the life-force spent by one is not, however, equivalent to the energy expended by another. It thus remains for Science to ascertain a rule by which the energy of one may be equitably exchanged for the energy of another in order to absolutely prove the perfect justice and practicability of the Socialistic maxim —"the time and service of one man is equivalent to equal time and service of any other."

Such a rule, discovered and applied in practice upon Socialistic foundations, ensures forever the first economic law of justice, that if a man toil not neither shall he eat.

Has that rule been discovered ? Yes. And so simple is it that a well-worn phrase comprises it all. That phrase is : "Cost is the limit of price."

A producer is entitled to receive in exchange for the life-force expended by him in producing an article any other article or articles upon which an equal amount of life-force has been expended by any other producer.

In order to measure this life-force an unvarying standard should be adopted. That standard should be the average life of the worker in the occupation where the labor requires the expenditure of the least life-force per hour.

For example, let us say that that work is clerical work. Statistics being taken in every trade and every locality, it is found, let us say, that a clerk in Berlin is able to work for forty years four hours a day, that a shoemaker in Berlin is only able to work thirty years, and that a knife-grinder is only able to work twenty years. Were all these people paid equally at so much an hour, everybody would want to be a clerk and nobody would be a knife-grinder. If the hour of the knife-grinder was held equal to the hour of the clerk it would be injustice, for there is no real equality between them. The knife-grinder by working his whole life would only be able to obtain two-thirds of the product of the shoemaker or one-half of the product of the clerk, whereas the products of all three should be of equal value and interchangeable. The knife-grinder being only able to work twenty years upon the life energy he possesses, or one-half the time of the clerk, should be credited for every hour's work with two hours, the shoemaker with one and one-third hour, and the clerk with but one hour. This would be absolute justice. Nothing else would.

Let the statistics—facts—be gathered in every trade and in each locality; from them, and from them alone, can the true cost and consequent just price for any production be learned. Nature, science, and common sense are the founders, discoverers, and promulgators of this law: let not the loafers much longer defy it.

The time-book system of Mr. T. F. Hagerty is the only device of which I have ever read that would carry it into practice and successful operation. In brief, that system is this:

Given: a Socialistic system wherein all production and distribution is done by the "Government" (the whole people in co-partnership). Given as incidents thereof: in San Francisco its proper quota of manufactories where goods are made and marts where they are sold. Here follows the result:

John Brown, a metal worker, presents himself at the machine-shop and asks for work. The foreman sets his task for him and notes the time at which he goes to work. John Brown quits when he pleases, works one hour or ten as suits his own will, only taking care that when he does quit the foreman marks upon the factory day-book and upon John Brown's own pass-book the number of hours that he has been at work. This pass-book is issued to John Brown by the County Clerk. It contains his photograph, his personal description and blank leaves thereafter for debit and credit account. At the top of these blank pages is printed :

JOHN BROWN.

In account with Socialistic Republic, the People of the United States.
Dr.   Cr.

Upon the credit side hereof the foreman makes this entry :

Jan. 2 : By labor ....6 hrs. 30 m.

On subsequent days he makes other entries, so that on Saturday night John Brown's credit page reads as follows :

JOHN BROWN.

In account with the Socialistic Republic, the People of the United States.
Cr.

In Machine Shop No. 22,961.

			hrs.	min.
Jan. 2 :	By labor		6	30
" 3 :	"	"	7	20
" 4 :	"	"	10	0
" 5 :	"	"	3	15
" 6 :	"	"	4	20
" 7 :	"	"	5	10
	Total for the week		36	35

Saturday afternoon he desires to make his purchases for the support of his family for the coming week.

He goes to the Government grocery marts. He asks the price of a sack of flour. The clerk in charge refers to the figures upon the sack. These read : one hour and twenty minutes. The clerk explains that this is the average time which it has taken farmer, miller, bag-maker, transporter, and storage clerk to produce and place on sale this article. It is not necessary for him to affirm that it is of the best quality, full weight, and un-adulterated. That is an uncontested fact, since the Government does not deal in shams. Brown takes the flour and passes over his time-book to the clerk, who enters upon the debit side the charge, entering it also upon the day-book of the store.

The package is marked with Brown's address and set aside for delivery at his house by the Government goods-carrier.

In a similar manner Brown makes whatever other purchases he desires. At the close of them all the debit page of his book reads as follows :

		hrs.	min.
Jan. 8. To goods bought		1	20
" "		4	
" "		5	
" "		3	
" "			20
" "			40
" "		1	20
Total		15	40

	hrs.	min.
By labor done	36	35
To goods bought	15	40
Time on hand	20	55

This "time on hand" John Brown can spend in the future, can keep in reserve for emergencies, lay up for days of sickness or laziness as he chooses.

This is the time-book system in brief. Under its operation for the first time in the history of the world would the worker be able to secure the FULL value of his labor. B. G. H.

APPENDIX B.

LABOR PAPERS.

As in some measure indicating the strength of the movement we append a list of the journals in the United States which are, wholly or in part, devoted to the great cause of the proletariat :

SOCIALISTIC.—*Truth*, the English Organ, a monthly magazine, Editor Burnette G. Haskell, San Francisco. *The Labor Enquirer*, English weekly, Editor Joseph R. Buchanan, Denver, Col. *Examiner*, English weekly, Hartford, Conn. *Sociologist*, English monthly, Knoxville, Tenn. *New Yorker Volks-Zeitung*, German daily and weekly, New York City. *Arbeiter-Zeitung*, German daily and weekly, Chicago, Ill. *Tageblatt*, German daily and weekly, Philadelphia. *Freiheit*, German weekly, New York City. *Vorbote*, German weekly, Chicago. *Der Fackel*, German weekly, Chicago. *Der Neue Tid*, Scandinavian weekly, Chicago. *Proletar*, Bohemian weekly, New York. *The Free Soiler*, monthly, New York City. *Boudoucnost*, Bohemian weekly, Chicago. *Journal of United Labor*, official English fortnightly organ of the Knights of Labor, Philadelphia, Pa. *The Protest*, English weekly, Exeter, N. H.

SEMI-SOCIALISTIC. — *John Swinton's Paper*, English weekly, New York City. *Man*, English weekly, New York City. *The Truth Seeker*, English weekly, New York City. *The Radical Review*, English weekly, Chicago, Ill. *Lucifer*, English weekly, Valley Falls, Kan. *The Non-Conformist*, English weekly, Tabor, Ia. *The Daily Laborer*, English daily, Haverhill, Mass. *The Advertiser*, English weekly, Hayes Valley, San Francisco.

Mail, daily, Stockton, Cal.   *Palladium of Labor*, Hamilton, Ontario.

SOCIALISTICALLY INCLINED.—*Labor Herald*, Pittsburg, Pa. ; *Vidette*, Salem, Oregon. ; *Labor Standard*, Paterson, N. J. ; *Advertiser*, Trenton, N. J. ; *Labor Free Press*, Baltimore, Md. ; *Craftsman*, Washington, D. C. ; *Union*, St. Louis, Mo. ; *Irish World*, New York City—all English weeklies.

APPENDIX C.

DECLARATION OF THE RIGHTS OF MAN.

[OFFICIAL.]

HEADQUARTERS EXECUTIVE PACIFIC COAST DIVISION,
INTERNATIONAL WORKMEN'S ASSOCIATION,
SAN FRANCISCO, CALIFORNIA.

The following " Declaration of the Rights of Man " is ordered published to the people :

PREAMBLE.

We hold these truths to be self-evident to all people who have the welfare of humanity at heart : That all men and women are born free and with equal rights. That they were endowed, by such birth, by their Creator, and as necessary incidents of their existence, with certain inalienable rights, rights of which even they cannot divest themselves ; and that among these rights are the right to life and the means of living, liberty and the conditions essential to liberty, and the right to the pursuit of happiness. That especially enumerating the subordinate rights flowing naturally and reasonably from the establishment of these truths and the principles necessary for their perpetuity, we do publish and declare :

I.

That the just end of all political associations and the only permissible reason for their existence at all, is the maintenance of the natural and imprescriptible rights of man and the development of all his faculties.

II.

Whatever rights belong to one man belong to all men equally, whatever difference there may be in their physical, mental, or moral force. Equality of rights is established by nature. Society, so far from invading it, ought justly to constitute a security against the abuse of force which would render it illusory.

III.

If it should be found, after careful trial thereof, that any form or system of government or society fails to maintain the rights of man, then it is not only the right but the most sacred duty of the whole people to alter or abolish the said system by any and all possible means.

IV.

Liberty is the power which belongs to a man of exercising all his faculties at pleasure. It has justice for its rule, the rights of others for its boundaries, nature for its origin, and the law for its safeguard.

V.

The right of life, which belongs equally to all men, carries with it the right to the means of living. Chief among these subsidiary rights is the right of each individual to receive the full product of his own labor, without tithe, tax, or diminution, upon any pretext.

VI.

Every individual is entitled to an equal proportional share of all the natural advantages of earth. The whole people should hold the land, light, air, and water, together with other of nature's resources, as the natural heritage in common of all mankind, and of his proportion thereof no man should ever be deprived.

VII.

Every individual is entitled to an equal proportionate share of all the accumulated wealth created by past generations, and that wealth should be held by society as the natural heritage in common of all mankind.

VIII.

Society can deny to those who do not consent to this system of society any share of the benefits produced by the co-operation of those who do consent. It is but just that those who will not co-operate should receive none of the benefits of co-operation.

IX.

Debt, profit, interest, rent, and the competitive system of industry are hereby formally declared proved instruments of degradation and tyranny, and cancers upon the social body. So also are the present methods of punishing crime rather than preventing it ; the present monetary system ; the present method of suffrage ; the present method of education ; and the present systems of jurisprudence, church and military.

X.

The right of peaceably assembling ; of manifesting opinion, whether through the press or by any other means ; of the free exercise of religion ; of bearing arms ; of security of person against unreasonable search or seizure, and of complete liberty of thought and speech, together with the right of association, are such necessary consequences of the principles of man's liberty, that the necessity of declaring them presupposes either the presence of, or the recent remembrance of, despotism.

XI.

The right of private property can justly be based upon no principle except that of having been produced by the person in possession of it, or upon the possessor having rendered for it the full equivalent to the one who did produce it. This rule can have no exceptions save those created by the unanimous consent of all members of society.

XII.

So long as members of society shall fulfil their portion of the social contract they have a right to demand of society the means necessary to provide for their subsistence. Society is bound also to insure the means of existence to those who are incapable of labor.

XIII.

Absolute justice is the right of every being. The law is the free and solemn expression of the public will, and it must be equal for all. Society ought to favor with all its power the progress of public reason, and place instruction and recreation within the reach of every citizen. The people is the sovereign. Government is its work and its property ; the public functionaries are its agents and officers, and the people justly should have the power when it pleases to revoke its mandatories or recall its servants. The law can forbid only what is hurtful to the people, and can prescribe only what is useful. Every law which violates or infringes the imprescriptible right of man is void.

XIV.

In every just government the law ought above all to defend public and individual liberty against the authority of those that govern. Every institution that does not suppose the people good and the magistrate corruptible, is vicious. No part of the people can exercise the power of the whole people ; but the wish it expresses ought to be respected as a wish of a part of the people which is to concur in forming the general will. Every act against the imprescriptible rights of man, by whomsoever exercised, even in the name of the law itself and within the forms it prescribes—every such act is arbitrary and void. The very respect due to law forbids submission to it, and if the attempt be made to execute such act by violence or by artifice, it is not only permitted but enjoined upon every individual to repel such assaults, even by force. Resistance to oppression is a necessary consequence of the other rights of man. There is oppression against the social body whenever one alone of its members is oppressed. There is oppression against every member of it when the social body is oppressed. When the government violates the rights of the people, insurrection is for the people, and for every portion of the people, the most sacred of rights and the most indispensable of duties. When the social contract fails to protect a citizen he resumes his natural right to defend personally all his rights. In either of the two preceding cases, to subject to legal forms the resistance to oppression is the last refinement of tyranny, and is both infamous and void.

XV.

Public functions cannot be considered as distinctions nor as recompenses, but as public duties. The people ought, as far as possible, to govern themselves without the interposition of delegates or representatives. But when these representatives are necessary they must be selected by such a system as will insure their being real and not pretended microcosms of their constituents. The crimes of such representatives should be severely punished. The people have a right to know the operations of their delegates, and it is the duty of the latter to render to the people a faithful account of their behavior.

XVI.

Men of all countries are brothers, and the people of each ought to yield one another mutual aid, according to their ability, like citizens of the same state. He who opposes or oppresses one people is the declared enemy of all. Those who make war on a people to arrest the progress of liberty and to annihilate the rights of man ought to be pursued everywhere, not as ordinary criminals but as social outlaws, assassins, and robbers. Kings, aristocrats, tyrants of every description are beasts dangerous to the welfare of mankind, and against them should be raised the hand of every man.

XVII.

The conditions which will establish universal happiness upon earth consist in the free enjoyment of the natural rights of man, combined with the exercise of all his faculties upon the highest plane of mental, moral, and physical worth. The best guarantee of the existence and perpetuity of these conditions is the loftiest possible elevation of humanity. There will arrive a time, if progress be not impeded, when governments will be useless. To advance that time, education seems to be the main factor. Hence, what prevents or constrains the spread of intelligence is tyrannous and unjust.

XVIII.

Governments, as at present existing, are machines used for the purpose of enslaving the people. Such machines should be abolished and society be permitted to reorganize upon principles of equality. The people being too much governed, all statute or common law, except broad and simple declarations of principles and rights, should be abolished. These principles should be interpreted, not by infamous precedent, but by the light of common sense, to secure justice to all.

XIX.

Neither sex, age, color, nor condition should ever be made barriers against equal and exact justice.

XX.

Suppress the *right of increase* claimed by the proprietor over anything which he has stamped as his own (property) while maintaining *possession*, and by this simple change, law, government, economy, and institutions will be revolutionized and evil be driven from the face of the earth.

DECLARATION.

We believe firmly that, as a necessary step in advance to that condition of perfect "an-archy" when governments shall be no longer needed, it is imperative that the present competitive system of industry and the social structure dependent thereon be abolished, and that in its place shall be substituted a system of governmental co-operation in all matters of mental, moral, and physical construction and elevation.

We believe in the fact that the present system necessarily is prophetic of a future revolution, which must either result in a greater and freer condition, or will plunge our present civilization back into barbarism.

We affirm that, believing this, it is our duty to prepare for the impending conflict; to lead it when it shall break upon us, and to bend every energy to so direct it as to secure as its result the establishment of a proper system of governmental co-operation.

We affirm, furthermore, that all the resources of science should be enlisted in the battle to insure success and the welfare of the people of the world.

We declare further that action ought to be both international and simultaneous.

It will be remembered that in 1872, at the Congress of the International held at the Hague, first arose the dissensions which have since divided our ranks. It was at that session that Bakounine was expelled, and carried with him thirty of the delegates, with the aid of whom he established what has since been called the Black International, as opposed to those who remained, the Red. The belief of the Red was in the gradual education of the people and in taking no forcible action until all the world was prepared ; the belief of the Blacks was in the total abolition of all present forms of government by force.

The news of this division when brought to Bismarck provoked from him this historical remark : " Crowned heads, wealth, and privilege well may tremble should ever again the Black and the Red unite ! "

There exists now no great obstacle to that unity. The work of peaceful education and revolutionary conspiracy well can and ought to run in parallel lines.

The day has come for solidarity. Ho ! Reds and Blacks, thy flags are flying side by side ! Let the drum beat out defiantly the roll of battle, " Workingmen of all lands, unite ! You have nothing to lose but your chains ; you have a world to win ! "

Tremble ! oppressors of the world ! Not far beyond your purblind sight there dawns the scarlet and sable lights of the JUDGMENT DAY.

Published by order of Division Executive.

1–41, Division Secretary.

The International Workmen's Association, organized August 5, 1862, at London, England.

The names and addresses of correspondents in Europe are for obvious reasons suppressed. The Central Executive and all divisions elsewhere can be reached by letter addressed in care of this Division.

The Bureau of Information, North American Section, can be addressed by letter, through the Secretary, " 1–41," 1236 Twenty-first Street, San Francisco, California.

The International's Method of Organization—The Group System.

Let us suppose that you, my reader, have been giving a little attention to the sayings and doings of the labor men ; that you have read and thought sufficiently on the subject to have a pretty good general idea of their principles and aims, and that you find yourself more or less in accord with them ; that still you entertain some objections and difficulties and your mind is in a condition of doubt and uncertainty. Now, let us suppose you to have among your acquaintances two or three persons similarly disposed, and that you invite them to meet you expressly to talk over the subject. Suppose that, as the result of your first meeting, you are all sufficiently interested to wish to meet for the same purpose again and again, sometimes in the apartments of one and sometimes in those of the others. Finally you meet regularly—say once a week—and from two or three your numbers have increased to half a dozen or more. In the meantime you have obtained for yourselves, and have read and discussed together, or passed from one to another, some labor literature. Perhaps, also, you have thrown yourself into intercourse with some well-informed labor advocate.

Now, my reader, I will venture to say that the desire which you first had to study the subject, for your own sake, will have expanded by this time into a desire to spread your views everywhere within the circle of your influence, and the same desire will animate your companions. Suppose, then, that each of you, while retaining your organization as a little club—a "group"—should make himself the starting point or nucleus of just such another club or "group," composed of persons perhaps living in his immediate neighborhood, or associated in business, or in some other way. The formation of these secondary clubs or groups, and this development, will be easier than that of the first, as each will have the advantage of an intelligent teacher. You see that in a very short time, instead of *one* you will have *eight* little clubs or groups, each having a thread of communication with the first one, which will continue to hold its regular meetings. Within another short period these eight clubs—meeting, perhaps, in different wards or suburbs of the city, or in little centres of rural population—will each in like manner make of its members the nuclei of other groups or clubs, and each of these again of still others ; and so on *ad infinitum.*

This is the system of organization adopted by the International. Bear in mind that it is for educational purposes only.

Up to this point it will be seen that this method of

organization is very simple and quite natural ; it is also free from any expense for halls and advertising, and no constitution or by-laws or other formality is at all necessary. The time usually spent in society meetings in what is called "regular business" is entirely saved. As the meetings are quite informal, and probably held near the home of each member, there will be no inconvenience in attending them. Another advantage is—and this is an advantage that belongs to only very small associations—namely, that each club will probably be composed of persons of about the same class and habits and quite familiar with each other, there will be no timidity about the expression of individual opinion ; instead of half a dozen talkers and fifty listeners, every one will be a talker and every one a listener, and of course all will be thereby more interested and become more intelligent, and a real friendship will be likely to spring up between them. The reciprocity of thought will produce that effect. Another important advantage is, that there will be little likelihood of any one member assuming such authority as to become a "boss," a self-constituted incarnation of the society, making in its name all sorts of arrangements. Nearly all the present political associations are pestered and damaged by such ambitious or unprincipled individuals, and it is an evil of the first magnitude.

Each man is a member of one group which is under the chairmanship of its organizer. He is a simple member here, but if he desires himself to become an organizer he can do so by going out and organizing a group of his own.

Among the chief objects of the International is the ascertaining of the individual opinion of each of the members upon all questions of interest. Each member is expected to forward his views and thoughts and all information he obtains to headquarters.

The International has here already an extended organization, and has laid the foundation in many neighborhoods and over a continually widening district, of a really formidable association.

In this way, if every sympathizing reader of this article will set to work, it will be readily seen how quickly and successfully—supposing the ideas to be correct and the times ripe for them—the party may spread, like the ganglions of the nervous system, throughout the whole of this broad land, preparing public opinion, in advance of the crisis, for the new social order, and thus serving not only to mitigate the violence of the transition, but also to make the outcome of the new system of society more sure and satisfactory.

And, be it observed, that with this system there will be no necessity for any centralized authority or arbitrary regulation. Every little group will be independent and self-regulating, and will have the benefit of connection through its first member or founder with a group older than itself, and will thus be kept informed of the general movement of thought and the progress of the party elsewhere.

But the chief beauty of the plan is that a course of education has been mapped out and excellent text-books provided, and that these are placed in the hands of various groups, who forming themselves thus into classes are enabled, in an extremely short time, to perfectly familiarize themselves with the fundamental principles of true social science.

Following this course comes a scientific and comprehensive course of chemistry. In brief, the producers are scientifically elevated from the condition of ignorant slaves to the position of intelligent freemen, prepared to act as leaders in the great social revolution, whose birth throes are already agitating the world.

Secret, mysterious, world-wide, quietly honey-combing society, the I. W. A. offers to the daring and devoted men and women of earth, the sole practical means of releasing the wealth-producers from the shackles of tyranny. It does not fear betrayal, since its system of organization prevents the possibility of treason. It does not fear suppression, because it has millions of members, as well qualified as the leaders to assume direction should those now at the head be removed.

It does not fear failure, because it knows its own power and strength, and the justice and truth of its cause.

Suppose that you call together eight of your friends some evening this coming week at your own house.

Read them this article, then form yourselves into a group according to the above plan. Then forward an account of your meeting to the Division Secretary. You will then receive proper documents, and each man of the group can go out and organize a group of his own, and so on. Let us take, say a limit of three months, to perfect each group. If you alone should follow out the plan, what would be the result? Let us see : In the first series of groups there would be yourself and eight others, 9 ; In the second series, 72 ; In the third series, 648 ; In the fourth series, 5,832. That is to say that the ball thus set in motion by you alone would within one year organize effectively nearly six thousand men.

It is work of this kind that has undermined all the thrones of Europe, and which in but a few years more will make American workmen ready to clasp hands with their brothers in other lands, to topple to its fall the whole mighty incubus of wrong that now threatens the whole world with death and desolation.

www.ingramcontent.com/pod-product-compliance
Lightning Source LLC
Chambersburg PA
CBHW032358280326
41935CB00008B/619